MEMOIR OF SARAH B. JUDSON

MEMOIR OF SARAH B. JUDSON

OF THE AMERICAN MISSION TO BURMAH

BY

EMILY C. JUDSON

WITH NOTES BY THE AUTHOR

CURIOSMITH

MINNEAPOLIS

Published by Curiosmith.
Minneapolis, Minnesota.
Internet: curiosmith.com.

Previously published as: *Memoir of Sarah B. Judson of the American Mission to Burmah*, by Emily C. Judson. A New Revised Edition with Notes by the Author. New York: Sheldon & Company, Publishers, 498 & 500 Broadway, 1868.

ISBN 9781946145642

CONTENTS

CONTENTS *(Continued)*

PREFACE

It has occurred to me, in glancing over the little narrative I have prepared, that those friends of Mrs. Judson who have kindly furnished copies of her verses, may be disappointed at seeing so few of them selected for use. Readers of another class will regret that more of the minute particulars of her missionary-life are not given; as, the precise number of schools in which she was at different times engaged, her efforts for individual conversion, etc. etc. Others again, will recollect the letters which were so interesting to them, and, forgetting that very few can read them with *their* eyes and hearts, will wonder that such pleasant memorials of her they loved should not be placed within the reach of all.

To each of these I would reply, that in taking a view of her whole life, my first aim has been to preserve the nice balance, the faultless symmetry of her character; to present her as she appeared under all circumstances—the Woman and the Christian. And, in the second place, I have thought it not amiss to pay some regard to brevity. She had a poetic eye and heart—a genial love for the flowers, the streams, the stars, the beautiful in nature, and whatever is pure and elevated in man—but she was not a *mere* poetess. As a Christian, she was most ardently attached to the service which occupied so large a portion of her life; but it would be unjust to represent her in the light of a *mere* missionary. If she had left a journal, however, many interesting circumstances, now buried in the grave with her, would doubtless have been elicited; and her missionary course might have been more distinctly traced.

The peculiar character of her letters has been mentioned elsewhere; but in recurring to them here, it may be proper to remark, that names and dates have been usually omitted, because the quotations are so short and frequent that their insertion would give the page the air of a chronological table. For brevity's sake, I have taken the liberty, in two or three instances, of incorporating a quotation from one letter with some sentence from another on the same subject; and have sometimes dropped a clause having no direct bearing on the point which I wished to elucidate. Entire letters, however, stand precisely as she wrote them.

Yet another reason may be added for having introduced her poems so sparingly. Unfinished as they were, they did not meet the approval of her own cultivated taste; and, after she left America, none were ever published by her permission. My selections have usually been made with reference to some circumstance in her life; and, among the various copies of these in my possession, I have of course preferred that which seemed in my own judgment the best.

Rangoon, June 1st, 1847.

THE SUBJECT

SARAH BOARDMAN JUDSON, was born at Alstead, in the State of New Hampshire, Nov. 4, 1803. She was the eldest child of Ralph and Abiah Hall, who still survive her, and at present reside in Skaneateles, in the State of New York. While Sarah was but a child, her parents removed from Alstead to Danvers, and subsequently to Salem, in the State of Massachusetts. In the latter place she received her education and continued to reside, until she was married to the Rev. George Dana Boardman, July 4, 1825, with whom she embarked the same month for the East Indies, to join the American missionaries in Burmah. After residing some time at Calcutta and Maulmain, they settled in Tavoy, April 1, 1828. During her residence in Calcutta and Tavoy she had three children, of whom one only, George Dana Boardman, Jr., born August 18, 1828, survives her. She lost her husband Feb. 11, 1831, and was married again to Adoniram Judson, of Maulmain, April 10, 1834. At Maulmain she became the mother of eight children, of whom five survive her. After the birth of her last child, in Dec., 1844, she was attacked with chronic diarrhoea, from which she had suffered much in the early part of her missionary life. When in the progress of the disease, it became evident that nothing but a long voyage and an entire change of climate could save her life, she embarked with her husband and three elder children for America, April 26, 1845. The voyage was at first attended with encouraging results, but finally proved unavailing; and she departed this life on ship-board, in the port of St. Helena, Sept. 1, 1845.

A. J.

Chapter 1

EARLY DAYS

"Well, let it be, through weal and woe,
Thou know'st not now thy future range,
Life is a motley, shifting show,—
And thou a thing of hope and change."
—*Joanna Baillie.*

There are many persons yet living, that have a distinct remembrance of a fair young girl, who years ago had her home in the pleasant town of Salem, Massachusetts. She came thither, (to use her own pretty words, penned in early childhood) from among "beautiful groves, orchards filled with fruit trees, and gently gliding streams;" and she expresses, in the same connection, some dissatisfaction with exchanging all these pleasant things, for "nothing but houses and steeples." If you question those who have her portrait in their hearts, they will speak of faultless features, molded on the Grecian model; of beautifully transparent skin; warm, meek, blue eyes; and soft hair, "brown in the shadow, and gold in the sun." But affection has garnered up memories of so much greater richness, that you can learn nothing of these things, except upon inquiry. The little girl was no favorite of fortune, (that is, fortune on the golden side) for there were many mouths to feed in her father's house, and the means were scanty. She was the eldest of thirteen sons and daughters; and while those nearest her own age were yet in the cradle, the stern lesson was begun, and little Sarah became inured to toil and care. A tiny manuscript volume, traced in carefully-formed characters, almost the only relic of her busy childhood, lies beside me as I write; and although there are no complainings on its pages, there are words which give us, in simple sentences, whole tales replete with meaning. "My mother cannot spare me to attend school this winter; but I have begun this evening to pursue my studies at home." Again, the ensuing spring: "My parents are not in a situation to send me to school this summer; so I must make every exertion in my power to improve at home." These entries, made in a miniature day-book, at an age when few children can frame a correct sentence, bring before us a series of struggles, which affection may be allowed to contemplate with a proud sorrow. A mind less richly endowed must have sunk to the level of daily toil; but not so hers. Though shrinkingly modest, she had yet an elasticity of spirit, an inner vigor and hopefulness which, all silently, buoyed her up, and pushed her onward; and to this she gradually added habits of patient industry and quiet endurance. Improvement—intellectual improvement, was at this time the one grand object, apart from the performance of the duties of the day, which occupied her entire attention, the nucleus of thought and action. A few years later than the date of the little day-book, we find in a note to a friend the following suggestion: "I feel very anxious to adopt some plan for our mutual improvement. I think it might be useful for us to write to each other frequently; and let the subject be something from the Holy Scriptures. You select some passage which is not easily comprehended, and send it to me for explanation. I will consult commentators, and write what I think of it, and will send you a text in return. I think the advantages of such a correspondence will be numerous; it will serve to strengthen our friendship, teach us to express our ideas with propriety, and, what is still more important, make us better acquainted with the Word of God."

Care always regulates and balances a character, by bringing sober thoughtfulness; and it will be seen from the above extract, that Sarah was already thoughtful; indeed, we find evidence of this at twelve years of age, when she very naively remarks, "Tomorrow will be the day which is *called* Thanksgiving, but I have some fear, that it is *only in the name.*" Then, after making several remarks, which prove her to be no enemy to this pumpkin pie and roast turkey festival, she adds: "But this year I will try to be truly thankful, and not forget the good God who so kindly watches over my youthful days."

Much of her early poetry evinces the same disposition, for though not decidedly religious, it is on religious topics, mostly versification of Scripture scenes. In a large mass of tattered fragments, I find a Scripture poem of several cantos in length, which must have been written at a very early age, and never copied, probably never finished. It is very difficult to decipher it in anything like a connected form; but a fine passage may be gleaned here and there—fine, when the writer's age and advantages are remembered—in which we cannot but discover unusual promise. The following description of the Israelites, as they encamped by the waters of Elim, bears no date, except such as may be gathered from the cramped autography, which, in its prim, stiff neatness, bears a strong resemblance to the little day-book already mentioned.

"Slowly and sadly, through the desert waste,
The fainting tribes their dreary pathway traced;
Far as the eye could reach th' horizon round,
Did one vast sea of sand the vision bound.
No verdant shrub, nor murmuring brook was near,
The weary eye and sinking soul to cheer;
No fanning zephyr lent its cooling breath,
But all was silent as the sleep of death;
Their very footsteps fell all noiseless there,
As stifled by the moveless, burning air;
And hope expired in many a fainting breast,
And many a tongue e'en Egypt's bondage blest.

Hark! through the silent waste, what murmur breaks?
What scene of beauty 'mid the desert wakes?
Oh! 'tis a fountain! shading trees are there,
And their cool freshness steals out on the air!
With eager haste the fainting pilgrims rush,
Where Elim's cool and sacred waters gush;
Prone on the bank, where murmuring fountains flow,
Their wearied, fainting, listless forms they throw;
Deep of the vivifying waters drink,
Then rest in peace and coolness on the brink.
While the soft zephyrs, and the fountain's flow,
Breathe their sweet lullaby in cadence low.
Oh! to the way-worn pilgrim's closing eyes,
How rare the beauty that about him lies!
Each leaf that quivers on the waving trees,
Each wave that swells and murmurs in the breeze,
Brings to his grateful heart a thrill of bliss,
And wakes each nerve to life and happiness.
When day's last flush had faded from the sky,
And night's calm glories rose upon the eye,
Sweet hymns of rapture through the palm-trees broke,
And the loud timbrel's deep response awoke;
Rich, full of melody, the concert ran,
Of praise to God, of gratitude in man,
While, as at intervals, the music fell,
Was heard, monotonous, the fountain's swell,
That, in their rocky shrines, flowed murmuring there,
And song and coolness shed along the air;
Night mantled deeper, voices died away,
The deep-toned timbrel ceased its thrilling sway;
And there, beside, no other music gushing,
Were heard the solitary fountains rushing,
In melody their song around was shed,
And lulled the sleepers on their verdant bed."

A versification of David's lament over Saul and Jonathan, is free from the defects of the piece quoted above, and faithful to the beautiful original. It is known to be one of the very earliest of her efforts, but it not unlikely received some improvements from the cultivated taste of later years:

The beauty of Israel for ever is fled,
And low are the noble and strong;
Ye children of music encircle the dead,
And chant the funereal song.

Oh, speak not in Gath of the mighty laid low!
Be ye mute in proud Askelon's street!
Their daughters, in triumph at Israel's woe,
With scoffs the sad tidings would greet.

Ye mountains of Gilboa, never may dew
At eventide visit your flowers;
May the fruits which the fields of your offerings strew,
Never welcome the soft summer showers.

While there, in his proud, princely beauty he stood,
Was the bow of the warrior unstrung;
And low in the shadows that darken thy wood
The shield of the mighty was flung.

Oh, stronger than young mountain lions were they!
Like the eagles they never knew fear;
And proud as they walked in their kingly array
Shone the light upon helmet and spear.

For Saul, oh, ye daughters of Israel most fair!
Who clothed you in scarlet and gold,

Untwine every gem from your beautiful hair,
And in sack-cloth your loveliness fold.

And I—oh, my brother! in sorrow for thee,
My spirit is bending full low!
Thy smiles and thy voice have been pleasant to me,
As the streams that in Lebanon flow.

Thy love was a wonderful, beautiful thing,
More than kindles in woman's fond breast;
Not thy sister's young arms to my neck as they cling,
More tenderly ever caressed.

Ye daughters of music, encircle the dead!
And chant the funereal song;—
The beauty, the glory of Israel have fled,
And low in the dust lie the strong.

Sarah's fondness for poetry was not only singular, but somewhat wonderful, as it had no incentives. The poetical talent cannot be developed without leisure; hence, though we often find it budding amid the common affairs of life, the sober, lowly pursuits by which we gain food and raiment, some mournful blight is sure to mar the expanding blossom, or its growth is cramped by petty cares. Our young songstress had no leisure; her hands and her thoughts were both continually busy; and, in after years, when her cares increased in magnitude, they did not diminish in number. She was busy to the end. When we compare the last mournful effusion of the dying wife with the above spirited effort of the young girl, we are prevented from wondering at the small improvement in style and finish, only, by its exquisitely touching tone, made melodious by the poetry of the spirit. But the wonder, were it awakened, would pass away, could we follow both child and woman along their laborious paths, and see the thoughts of the moment linked hastily in careless rhyme, as the hurried traveller binds, while he hastens onward, the nosegay, not too nicely culled, which he gathered by the wayside. But young Sarah did not merely lack leisure; she had no one to guide and prune, to suggest and encourage; her whole library of poetry consisted of a copy of Ossian, (which she versified almost as freely as she did the Scriptures) and Thomson's "Castle of Indolence." Yet it is impossible to examine her papers without feeling that she laid no common offering on the altar of her God, when she breathed the petition—"Here am I, send me!" With opportunities to ripen and improve, she would have been surpassed by few female poets in the world. But a better destiny, though one of many shadows, lay before her, and none can regret that she chose the soberer pathway.

At the age of seventeen, we find Sarah teaching for a few months, that she may gain the means of studying for the same length of time; and then, pursuing the laborious task of paying for the morning's recitation, by taking charge of a class of little girls during the remainder of the day, and no doubt poring over her books far into the night. We are accustomed to consider a self-educated man, with all his physical strength and multiplicity of resources, worthy of all praise; what, then, shall we say of the woman, who, unassisted and alone, goes beyond most of her sex, in accomplishing the same object. It is difficult to ascertain the extent of our young student's school education, but passages from letters to intimate friends tell something; and the degree of mental discipline which she brought to the performance of later duties, proves that her attainments were not superficial.

"We have finished Butler's Analogy since you left school, and are now taking lessons in Paley's Evidences."

"I am studying Campbell's Philosophy of Rhetoric."

"I am engaged this term in the study of Logic and Geometry."

"I am at home this winter, teaching my little brothers, and so have more leisure to devote to my Latin."

Thus, with a multiplicity of duties on her hands, was she toiling patiently along the upward path to mental superiority—preparing for still heavier, but most precious toil.

Chapter 2

A NEW LIFE

"Till David touched his sacred lyre,
In silence lay the unbreathing wire;
But when he swept its chords along,
Even angels stooped to hear the song.
So sleeps the soul till Thou, oh Lord!
Shall deign to touch its lifeless chord—
Till waked by Thee, its breath shall rise.
In music, worthy of the skies."

—*Moore.*

Of Sarah's early religious impressions I have learned but little, except that they were like those of most thoughtful children, sometimes strong, but always evanescent. Now she would appear excessively alarmed at the thought of death, and now seem utterly forgetful of her mortality; at one moment we find her distressed and tearful, and in the next all happiness, as though the earth were one vast flower, and she a butterfly, molded expressly to sip its sweets. But this could not continue, and at the age of sixteen there came a change—a spirit-birth. The "lifeless chord" was touched at last, and angels bent to hear the music. It was a melody which angels could appreciate; but it may yet find an echo in many a human bosom.

"I have this day," (June 4, 1820) "in the presence of the world, the holy angels, and the omniscient God, publicly manifested my determination to forsake the objects of earth, and live, henceforth, for Heaven. What have I done? Do I realize the importance of the step I have taken? Oh, my Saviour! I am weak, and the heart of man is deceitful; but I do hope in thy mercy. Thou didst die even for the chief of sinners, and I know thou wilt pardon all who come to thee believing. Take me, dear Saviour, all sinful, unworthy as I am—do with me what thou wilt, but oh! preserve me from wounding thy precious cause!"

"I have today wept tears of pity, I can almost say anguish, at the stupidity of sinners. Inhabitants of a Christian country, the word of God in their hands; the mild, compassionate Saviour waiting to receive them; the Spirit striving, and yet they bent upon their own destruction. But have I not more reason to be astonished and weep at my own coldness—I who have *felt*, that Jesus bled and died, even for *my* sins; *I* wander from the way of life! 'Turn me, oh God, and I shall be turned, draw me, and I shall run after thee.'"

"Today I had a long and serious conversation with my beloved sister Harriet. Sweet child! she wept when I told her of her dangerous state. I reminded her of the shortness of time, the certainty of death, the value of the soul, and the terrors of the Day of Judgment; and she appeared greatly distressed. But alas! I have reason to fear that her emotions were of a different nature from those I would fain excite. I know that she loves me tenderly, and apprehensions of an eternal separation cannot fail to give her pain. Oh! that the Holy Spirit might convince her, and convince my other sisters, and my brothers, of the importance of seeking an interest in the Saviour."

Behold the little missionary! her youthful feet tremblingly leaving their first impressions on the path of life, seizing upon the work nearest her, laboring and praying in the family circle—the true charity which "begins at home," and ends with the boundaries of the universe. But even then she did not think of home *merely;* and we may well believe that the shadow of her future life was, at that early period, flung back upon her spirit.

"It is my ardent desire," she writes to a friend, "that the glorious work of reformation may extend, 'till every knee shall bow' to the living God. For this expected, this promised era, let us pray earnestly, unceasingly, and with faith. How can I be so inactive, when I know that thousands are perishing in this land of grace; and millions, in other lands, are, at this very moment, kneeling before senseless idols."

But to return to the journal: a single sheet of paper folded as a little book, and the last that she ever kept. In less than a month after her baptism, she says: "While I have this day had the privilege of worshipping the true God in solemnity, I have been pained by thinking of those who have never heard the sound of the gospel. When will the time come that the poor heathen, now bowing to idols, shall own the living and true God? Dear Saviour, haste to spread the knowledge of thy dying love to earth's remotest bounds!"

"I have just completed the perusal of the life of 0; and never shall I forget the emotions of my heart, while following thus the footsteps of this devoted missionary. I have almost caught his spirit, and been ready to exclaim: Oh! that I, too, could suffer privations, hardships, and discouragements, and even find a watery grave, for the sake of bearing the news of salvation to the poor heathen! Then, I have checked myself in the wild, unreasonable wish. Sinners perishing all around me, and I, an ignorant, weak, faithless creature, almost panting to tell the far *heathen* of Christ! Surely, this is wrong. I will no longer indulge the vain, foolish wish, but endeavour to be useful in the position Providence has placed me. I can pray for deluded idolaters, and for those who labor among them; and this is a privilege indeed."

Ah, meek, true-hearted one! Such prayers as thine, through Him who never turns away from humble prayers, are the strength of many a human hand; and God grant that their pure incense may ever circle round the lone missionary of the Cross, and buoy up his spirit in the midst of toil, and privations, and the bitter, biting ingratitude of those who cannot understand the good it brings. Blessings on thy sweet, beautiful girlhood!—or blessings rather on its memories; for no blessings of ours can reach thee now, bright, sainted spirit that thou art! But the warmth, the humility, the deep devotedness, the whole graceful symmetry of thy lovely character—may it never be lost upon thy fair countrywomen!

With one more extract, the little journal must be closed. "When, dear Redeemer, when shall I be 'free from this body of sin and death?' I long to sit forever at thy feet, and gaze upon thy face. But, perhaps, before this happiness is mine, many a sorrowful, sinful day must be passed in this deceitful world. If so, I must not be impatient. Heaven is the place that I most desire; and should I *ever* be welcomed to its bliss, I shall be entirely satisfied. I ask only a heart to serve God, and labor for Him; and then, after living many years in this world, if I be admitted to the joys of heaven, sweet will be my rest."

Another glimpse of the manner in which Sarah, young as she was, commenced her "new life," may be gained, through the following to a friend. It is given as an apology for having neglected letter-writing. "I am deeply engaged in my studies, and my other avocations are numerous and imperious. Besides, I have been for six weeks past employed with a gentleman, upon the evidences of the soul's immortality, independent of the Scriptures. You may well believe that this subject has engrossed a large portion of my thoughts; and we have not yet finished the discussion."

An anecdote, illustrative of her faithful and yet engaging mode of reproval, is given by a friend, and called to mind by the above extract. At a house where Sarah was visiting, a young gentleman had left a pack of gaming cards upon the table. She saw them there, and wrote upon the envelope, "Remember now thy Creator in the days of thy youth; while the evil days come not, nor the years draw nigh, when thou shalt say, I have no pleasure in them." Startled, conscience-stricken, and curious, the gentleman made every effort to discover the source of the warning; and finally succeeded in engaging a mutual friend to convey a note of inquiry to the young monitress. She immediately replied:

"And would'st thou know what friend sincere,
Reminds thee of thy day of doom?

Repress the wish:—yet thou may'st hear,
She shed for thee a pitying tear,
For thine are paths of gloom."

Among the poems written about this time, are "Lines to my Pastor," "Thoughts on the Death of an Infant," "Why will ye die," etc. etc. But, except in the deep tone of religious feeling which characterizes most of them, they are in no wise superior to those of an earlier date. She was not yet eighteen, however, and there was too much of the real in her situation, to leave any great opportunity for the cultivation of the ideal. As a specimen of these productions, an extract may be taken from a short poem, entitled

GETHSEMANE

"Oh! black were the clouds which enveloped the even,
And slow from the hills crept the chill northern breeze,
Cold, cold were the dews, thick descending from heaven,
And hushed was each sound, save the rustling of trees.

On earth, gloom and sorrow together were blent,
When the Saviour of sinners, by anguish oppressed,
His sad, heavy steps to Gethsemane bent,
To breathe to his Father the griefs of his breast.

* * * * *

And can I, unmoved, hear those accents of woe?
The purple drop starting, with carelessness see?
From that measureless agony turn, and yet know,
Thus suffered the Saviour—*my* Saviour for me?

Then woe to this bosom! the bleak winds which blew
Through his locks, on that eve, as much tenderness felt;
Then woe to this bosom! 'tis cold as the dew,
And dull as the turf where in anguish he knelt."

It would be most interesting to be able to gain even the slightest glimpse of the path in which the young Christian walked for the few years immediately succeeding her public profession of religion—the heart-path, I mean—for the other is strewed with well-remembered acts. One lady will tell us of the female prayer-meeting, established in her chamber, just across the way, by this youngest member of the church; another may still possess the dear little tract which the meek young Christian walked a long, long way to drop at the door; and many, very many are there, who even at this late day think often of her words of gentle warning.

Mrs. C. C. P. Crosby, who has kindly furnished some valuable reminiscences, says, "My first *particular* acquaintance with Sarah Hall began in 1823, when she called on me, and invited me to join the Tract Society, and engage in distributing tracts in a certain district. At this time she was about eighteen years of age; and from that period till her departure for glory, the most affectionate intercourse was maintained. In the tract labors she was assiduously engaged during her residence in Salem. Soon after this event, (the call above mentioned) a few of her female friends indulged a trembling hope in the Saviour, and she succeeded in establishing a prayer-meeting, where she was accustomed to meet them each week for several months, and the happy results were, that all but one came forward publicly and put on Christ. Although the attendants on this meeting were all her seniors, and some of them married ladies, yet Miss Hall was the actual and acknowledged leader."

Her "pantings to tell the far heathen of Christ," and the self-upbraidings by which her singular humility strove to crush these aspirations, must have caused a struggle, on which those winged visitants, "sent to minister to the heirs of salvation," gazed with thrilling interest, but from us all is hidden. There are, indeed, some sweet lines, which give a slight evidence of a drawing of the heart westward; and containing a prophecy that,

"Ere long, in bright glory the gospel's pure light,

On each Cherokee dwelling shall shine;"

and we know, that at one time she had serious thoughts of becoming a member of the Indian Mission, in the West. Beside this, I have before me now, the torn fragment of a letter, apparently from the secretary of a missionary society in Central New-York, filled with inquiries respecting her qualifications to labor among the Oneidas; but to whom the letter was addressed, or what passed on the subject, I have no means of ascertaining. It serves to show, however, that her feet were already tending to the path, in which they were afterward to tread. The following lines, which are without date, treat of topics with which the heart seems to have been familiar:

COME OVER AND HELP US

"Ye, on whom the glorious gospel,
Shines with beams serenely bright,
Pity the deluded nations,
Wrapped in shades of dismal night,
Ye, whose bosoms glow with rapture,
At the precious hopes they bear;
Ye, who know a Saviour's mercy,
Listen to our earnest prayer!

See that race, deluded, blinded,
Bending at yon horrid shrine;
Madness pictured in their faces,
Emblems of the frantic mind;
They have never heard of Jesus,
Never to th' Eternal prayed;
Paths of death and woe they're treading,
Christian! Christian! come and aid!

By that rending shriek of horror,
Issuing from the flaming pile,

By the bursts of mirth that follow,
By that Brahmin's fiend-like smile,
By the infant's piercing cry,
Drowned in Ganges' rolling wave;
By the mother's tearful eye,
Friends of Jesus, come and save!
By that pilgrim, weak and hoary,
Wandering far from friends and home,
Vainly seeking endless glory
At the false Mahomet's tomb;
By that blind, derided nation,
Murderers of the Son of God,
Christians, grant us our petition,
Ere we lie beneath the sod!

By the Afric's hopes so wretched,
Which at death's approach shall fly;
By the scalding tears that trickle
From the slave's wild, sunken eye;
By the terrors of that judgement,
Which shall fix our final doom;
Listen to our cry so earnest;—
Friends of Jesus, come, oh, come!

By the martyrs' toils and sufferings,
By their patience, zeal, and love;
By the promise of the Mighty,
Bending from His throne above;
By the last command so precious,
Issued by the risen God;
Christians! Christians! come and help us,
Ere we lie beneath the sod!"

Chapter 3

THE CONSECRATION

"Behold her (life the offering)
In her young beauty bow;
There hear her quivering, glad lip breathe
Her consecration vow;
Love deathless, lighting up her eye,
Its glory on her brow."

In the year one thousand eight hundred and eighteen, the young, ardent, and devoted Colman first planted his eager foot upon the land of idols; and in little more than two short years, a grave was made for him in Chittagong. He did not go wearied and worn out with toil; but scarce had he raised one warning finger, scarce had he looked upon the field, when he was called from his morning labor, to the rest of the sainted. And there, beside his ashes, as though he had never been, the pagoda still stood undisturbed beneath the golden filigree of its own "umbrella," surrounded by a hundred miniature copies of its taper self; and still beneath the carved gables and glittering spires of the Kyoung, swarmed yellow-robed, indolent priests, pompously awake to their own importance, their sanctity and learning; but with all their cunning and their miserable pride, not a whit less ignorant and debased than their blinded worshippers. And thither, too, trooped thousands on thousands with their offerings—the old man with his fruit and rice, and the young girl with her flowers;—and when a few careless words had been muttered, with eye and heart both wandering, all thought that they had gained a step toward heaven, and went away to commit their daily sins without compunction, since "merit" could be again so cheaply bought. From this scene Colman passed, just as his tongue had learned to frame some broken, but precious sentences; and even the spirits above must have looked in wondering awe upon the strange dispensation, while awakened to new admiration of "the depth of the riches both of the wisdom and knowledge of God." On earth heavily sunk the sad intelligence into many a heart; for the mission cause was then in the weakness of its infancy; and to the finite eye, it looked a tottering cause, balanced on a single point.

Within the walls of Waterville College, on the green banks of the Kennebeck, sat a student poring over his books. His slight, though manly figure, gave no indication of physical strength; and there were blue veins on his temples, a flush upon his cheek, and at times a spiritual kindling of the eye, which formed a sad tablet, that the most careless might read with ease. It is seldom the destiny of one like him to count the allotted three score and ten links in the chain of life. But on the brow, and in the eye, and clustering about the pensively curved mouth, was a something full of promise, a high-toned devotedness of character, and a solemn earnestness, which seemed to say, that the chain might yet be all the richer for its shortness. To the student, in the midst of his books, came the voice of mourning; and with it, up from the ashes of the buried dead, came another voice, and his blue eye darkened, and his bosom swelled with enthusiasm, as he listened.

"A soldier has fallen! to the field! to the field!" fell the spirit-stirring call upon his heart; and though honors, such honors as a young man dearly loves to win, were waiting his acceptance; though bright visions lay before him, and loved ones gathered round, the voice still sounded in his ear, a trumpet-call, and he could not disobey. In solemn loneliness, the final consecration was at last made; and, in a few months more, young Boardman was an accepted missionary.

But the voice from the grave of Colman had reached a yet gentler spirit—a spirit as enthusiastic, as devoted, as noble as his own; but one which, in its meekness and feminine delicacy, could reply only by sorrowful harpings. Thus sung young Sarah Hall; and though by no means in her most poetical vein, there is a genuine heart-throb in every line.

"'Tis the voice of deep sorrow from India's shore,
The flower of our churches is withered, is dead,
The gem that shone brightly will sparkle no more,
And the tears of the Christian profusely are shed.
Two youths of Columbia, with hearts glowing warm,
Embarked on the billows far distant to rove,
To bear to the nations all wrapped in thick gloom,
The lamp of the gospel—the message of love.
But Wheelock now slumbers beneath the cold wave,
And Colman lies low in the dark, cheerless grave;
　　Mourn, daughters of Arracan, mourn!
　　The rays of that star, clear and bright,
　　That so sweetly on Chittagong shone,
　　Are shrouded in black clouds of night,
　　For Colman is gone!

At that sorrowful hour, that moment of woe,
When his cheek, lately glowing with health, was all pale;
And his lone wife, disconsolate, feeble and low,
Was sad, and no Christian replied to her wail;
Did not angels in sympathy shed the soft tear,
As they gazed from their thrones far beyond the blue sky?
Oh no; for the seraph of mercy was near,
To bid *him* rejoice, wipe the tear from *her* eye.
They saw, and with rapture continued their lays,
'How great is Jehovah! how deep are his ways!
　　The spirit of love from on high,

The hearts of the righteous hath fired;
Lo! they come, and with transport they cry,
We will go where our brother expired,
And labor and die.'

Oh, Colman! thy father weeps not on thy grave;
Thy heart-riven mother ne'er sighs o'er thy dust;
But the long Indian grass there most sweetly shall wave,
And the drops of the evening descend on the just;
Cold, silent, and dark is thy narrow abode,
But not long wilt thou sleep in that dwelling of gloom,
For soon shall be heard the great trump of our God,
To summon all nations to hear their last doom;
A garland of amaranth then shall be thine,
And thy name on the martyrs' bright register shine;
Oh, what glory will burst on thy view,
When are placed by the Judge of the earth
The flowers that in India grew
By thy care, on the never-pale wreath
Encircling thy brow!"

The elegy found its way to the public eye, and to the eye and heart of the student. Whence came it? where could the chord be hidden, whose tones gave so true an echo to that vibrating in his own bosom? Boardman was not a poet, and true gems of sentiment received little value in his eyes from the brilliancy of their setting; but by the light of his own soul, he read the high enthusiasm of another. At last they met, and, in the words of the only witness to that first meeting, "their spirits, their hopes, their aspirations, were one." And then, again, yet fonder, tenderer, though not stronger ties were broken, and beautiful was the living sacrifice laid on the altar.

Thrice difficult, at that day of few precedents, must have been such a self-consecration to a woman. Madness, the world calls it even now; and if treasure, if gold and diamonds, if earthly honors, if the fame which endures to the end of time, were the object, such madness would be too deep for measurement. Who, for any of these—what delicate, timid woman, would turn from the land of her birth to voluntary exile? Who, for these, could cast upon the roof which has sheltered her, the hearth-stone which has been wet with her tears, the walls which have rung with her childish laughter, the habitation which the smiles of the holiest earthly love have made precious by their sunlight—who could cast upon all these the abiding shadow which must needs darken all the places once blessed by her beloved presence? Who could look upon the mother who bore her, and whose arms are even then closed about her with that peculiar tenderness which has its birth only in a mother's bosom; upon the father, whose eye once lighted with pride at the sight of his darling, but is now dim with the blinding tears; the sister, the brother, who were the playmates of her childhood, and bosom friends of her youth—who could look into all these dear, fond, tearful faces, and then turn away her eyes and never look again? Who could cast away all the refinements of civilization, relinquish the sweet pleasures of social life, the beautiful associations, which cluster, like the spring-violets by her brook-sides, around every fair New England town—who could leave all these for a wilderness, where the glance of appreciation, the smile of sympathy, are never seen, where the refined, affectionate circle never gathers, and the Sabbath bell never sounds? For earthly treasure, none! none! But the Christian, she who knows that, in obedience to her Father's voice, she can never go beyond his smile—what has she to fear? What is the duty for which her spirit cannot be strengthened? Yet, none the less to her, is there anguish in such partings; and who can guess the additional heartache caused by one unkind or unwilling word. The first of these we are not told that Sarah was called to bear, farther than always falls upon those who turn aside from the common beaten track; but who, without more than Abraham's faith, could part willingly with such a child? and this faith was reserved to the last painful moment; for we have been told that poor Sarah received no encouragement from those she most loved, through all the indescribable, unimaginable struggles, anticipatory of the final self-sacrifice.

Mrs. Allen, in her beautiful obituary notice, contained in the Mother's Journal of December, 1845, says:

"If we mistake not, she had not at first the cordial consent of her family in this devotion of herself to a missionary life. She was a treasure too precious to be readily yielded up, even for this holy work. We recollect that when she left her paternal home, to reach the ship which was to convey her 'over the dark and distant sea,' after she had taken her seat in the stage-coach with her chosen companion, and the late revered Dr. Bolles, her pastor, and had bestowed her last farewell upon the family group—as though she felt that she had not obtained that free and full consent to her abandonment of home and country which her filial heart craved, she looked out at the coach window, and said, 'Father, are you willing? Say, father, that you are willing I should go.' 'Yes, my child, I am willing.' 'Now I can go joyfully!' was the emphatic response; and the noble wanderer went on her way with cheerful composure."

Of this scene Mrs. Boardman writes to her husband's parents, "My mother embraced me as tenderly, when she whispered, 'Sarah, I *hope* I am willing,' as she did one month before, when she wildly said, 'Oh! I cannot part with you!' Although my father's fond affection was very apparent, he still submissively acquiesced in what appeared to be the will of Providence. After we were seated in the carriage, I said, 'Papa, are you willing I should go?' 'Yes!' was the welcome reply."

And so the fond child's heart was made glad even in the moment of its agony; for something of the previous reluctance of the sorrow-stricken parents to resign their treasure may be gathered from such pleadings as these:

"Let us, my dear parents, go to Calvary; let us behold, for a few moments, the meek, the holy Lamb of God, bleeding for our transgressions. Then let us inquire, 'Shall I withhold from this Saviour any object, however dear to my heart? Shall I be unwilling to suffer a few short years of toil and privation for his sake? Let us call to remembrance those days of darkness through which we passed before Jesus lifted upon us the light of his countenance. We have, I trust, each of us, seen our lost and ruined condition by nature, have seen ourselves exposed to the righteous indignation of our Creator, have felt ourselves sinking into endless despair and ruin, and all this is merited. But oh, amazing love! at that desperate moment the Saviour smiled upon us. He opened his arms of compassion; all polluted as we were with iniquity, he received us, forgave our sins, and bade us hope for joy unutterable beyond the grave. Did we not, then, surrender *all* into his hand? Was not this the language of our hearts,

> 'Had I a thousand lives to give,
> A thousand lives should all be thine!'

And has not the precious Redeemer as strong claims upon us now as he had then?"

The sweet devotedness of her character, the forgetfulness of self, and thoughtfulness in regard to others, appear in beautiful relief through all these trials. She does not even say, "Why do ye weep, and break my heart." She speaks not a word of her own sufferings, but strives, with cheerful simplicity, to wipe away others' tears. "Give my love," she writes from Philadelphia, "to the dear children. Tell them, in a cheerful manner, that sister Sarah has gone to teach the poor little Burmans. I hope they will not be taught to associate sad ideas with my leaving them."

A short time previous to Sarah's marriage, she addressed the following plaintive lines to him who was soon to be her only earthly friend; and they are the only expression of any thought for herself which she has left:

> "When far from those whose tender care

Protected me from ills when young;
And far from those who love to hear
Affection from a sister's tongue;

When on a distant heathen shore,
The deep blue ocean I shall see;
And know the waves which hither bore
Our bark, have left me none but thee;
Perhaps a thought of childhood's days
Will cause a tear to dim my eye;
And fragments of forgotten lays
May wake the echo of a sigh.
Oh! wilt thou then forgive the tear?
Forgive the throbbings of my heart?
And point to those blest regions, where
Friends meet, and never, never part?

And when shall come affliction's storm,
When some deep, unexpected grief
Shall pale my cheek, and waste my form,
Then wilt thou point to sweet relief?

And wilt thou, then, with soothing voice,
Of Jesus's painful conflicts tell?
And bid my aching heart rejoice,
In these kind accents—*'All is well?'*
When blooming health and strength shall fly,
And I the prey of sickness prove,
Oh! wilt thou watch with wakeful eye,
The dying pillow of thy love?

And when the chilling hand of death
Shall lead me to my home in heaven,
And to the damp, repulsive earth,

In cold embrace, this form be given;

Oh, need I ask thee, wilt thou then,
Upon each bright and pleasant eve,
Seek out the solitary glen,
To muse beside my lonely grave?
And while fond memory back shall steal,
To scenes and days for ever fled;
Oh, let the veil of love conceal
The frailties of the sleeping dead.

And thou may'st weep, and thou may'st joy,
For 'pleasant is the joy of grief;'
And when thou look'st with tearful eye
To heaven, thy God will give relief.

Wilt thou, then, kneel beside the sod
Of her who kneels with thee no more,
And give thy heart anew to God,
Who griefs unnumbered for thee bore?
And while on earth thy feet shall rove,
To scenes of bliss oft raise thine eye,
Where, all-absorbed in holy love,
I wait to hail thee to the sky."

The Rev. Doct. Babcock, who had the pastoral charge of the church at Salem after the young missionary's departure, thus speaks of her as she was described to him by those who knew her well. "She had been remarkable, from the period of her first professing herself a disciple of Christ, for the symmetry and early maturity of her piety. This made her the object of attention and attraction among all the more spiritual-minded members of that lovely church. In the domestic circle, she was most useful, and indeed the chief dependence of parents well able to appreciate this inestimable jewel.

Their own very limited circumstances and numerous younger children, with the feebleness of her mother's health, threw on her young arms no trifling load. But with that quiet, native energy and perseverance which always characterized her, she contrived, after faithfully accomplishing the heavy tasks devolving on her at home, to find time and means for successful mental cultivation."

The editress of the Mother's Journal, in the obituary notice already mentioned, says farther:—"She was of about middle stature, agreeable in her personal appearance, and winning in her manners. The first impression of an observer respecting her, in her youth, at the time of her departure from the country, would be of a gentle, confiding, persuasive being, who would sweeten the cup of life to those who drank it with her. But further acquaintance would develop strength as well as loveliness of character. It would be seen that she could do and endure as well as love and please. Sweetness and strength, gentleness and firmness, were in her character most happily blended. Her mind was both poetical and practical; she had refined taste, and a love for the beautiful as well as the excellent."

For some years before she went to India, she had been a contributor to the Christian Watchman and Baptist Magazine, or had written several articles which found their way into these and other publications. Her poetry then had merit. A piece written upon the death of Messrs. Colman and Wheelock, soon after their arrival in Burmah as missionaries, and another upon the death of Catharine Brown, a Cherokee girl, attracted attention, and gave a favorable impression of the writer before she was otherwise known to the public.

It may not be amiss to insert in this connection, an Acrostic, (a somewhat fashionable style of compliment in New-England twenty-five years ago) addressed to the young poetess, previous to her acquaintance with Mr. Boardman. As it appeared anonymously in a newspaper, the author's name cannot be given with any degree of certainty, but there are some strong reasons for suspecting that it would be *now* no strange sound, in the ear of the readers of popular American literature.

SARAH HALL

"Soft and sweet thy numbers flow,
And with pious fervor glow;
Raptured, we thy strains admire,
And would catch thy hallowed fire;
Heavenly themes, and strains divine,
Blessed harmonist, are thine.
Happy songstress, tune thy lay,
Artless thus, till called away;
Loosed from earth to sing above
Lays divine, in realms of love."

What Sarah B. Hall would have been, if her young mind had not taken the self-denying direction, that prevented the literary development, to which she seemed at first inclined, may be the subject of agreeable conjecture; what she really was, we shall soon learn, by following her across the blue waters to her tropic home.

Chapter 4

CONTRASTS

"And there are men in uncouth dress,
That round the stranger vessel press;—
And fragrant groves on every side,
Bask in the sultry, noon-day beam,
Or lave their branches in the tide,
Of Arah-wah-tee's tranquil stream
But not a tree on all the strand,
Is known in Anna's native land."[1]

Ann Hasseltine Judson, as she appeared at Washington during the winter of 1823, is thus described by the Rev. Doct. Babcock: "Rather above the medium female stature, her pleasant, frank, open countenance had still an air of dignity, an ingenuous, unsought loftiness of bearing, which could not fail to inspire profound respect and almost a feeling of awe. Her conversation partook of the same traits. She was affable and meek, yet was she most emphatically dignified. . . . The whole impression produced by intercourse with her at this period, was that of majestic sweetness."

Others have spoken more minutely of a half-oriental style of beauty—a fine oval face, with a profusion of jetty curls around

1 From "Anna's Return"—a poem addressed to Mrs. Ann H. Judson, by a daughter of J. Butterworth, M. P. London.

it, rich Spanish complexion, and dark, deep eyes, full of the lofty enthusiasm of character, the latent heroism, afterwards so thrillingly developed. At Salem the two met—the brilliant, accomplished woman, who had studied the human heart, in its various phases, on three continents, and who by her innate loftiness, as well as high-toned devotedness of spirit, could awe both savage and cultivated minds; and young, timid Sarah Hall, an unsunned dew-drop, in her sweet meekness. How strangely interesting this meeting; if any there had but possessed the power to turn a few leaves in the book of human destiny!

A little anecdote will serve to illustrate a trait of character in the younger, which was prominent through life. True greatness, after it has once been developed, however unassuming, bears always with it a consciousness of power, perfectly consistent with feminine delicacy and Christian humility. Clothed in this power, sat the returned missionary, surrounded by listening admirers and learned divines, discussing topics of vast magnitude and weighty importance. Miss Hall, totally unaware of the wealth of thought and feeling as yet but partly unlocked in her own bosom, and blushing with girlish timidity whenever the fine, dark eye fell on her, endeavoured to shrink from observation, while she drank in every word with greedy earnestness. But the nature of the "consecration vow" she had breathed was no secret; and so her personality was gone, or at least that part of it which consisted in an indulgence of natural feeling, as well as that which would have made her the exclusive proprietor of the swellings of her own heart. I believe it is the opinion of wise men, that a woman daring enough to identify herself with one who is to stand on the outposts of Zion, should have no objection to occupying a kind of honorable pillory, before both church and world, till the curiosity of wondering gazers is fully satisfied; so, one who loved young Sarah well, but could not comprehend the delicate attunement of her spirit, made a startling proposition. What could be more interesting here, in the presence of one who had seen Colman in India, than the reading of the Elegy; and that by the fair author, now on the eve of following in his footsteps? Interesting to the *listeners*, of course; so despite her low pleadings, (for genuine modesty would not allow her to attract the attention of the waiting company by stronger demonstrations of reluctance) the poor, trembling girl was dragged before the awe-inspiring circle, and the paper thrust into her hand. One better versed in the ways of the world would have released herself from the embarrassing position with ease; and two years after so would she. But now she saw no mode of escape. She commenced reading in a hurried, faltering tone, quite unusual; but she, also, had enthusiasm of character, and a quiet dignity, and her soul had been in the subject when she wrote; so her voice gradually grew firm, and resumed its natural modulations. She finished, and without raising her head enough to perceive that the eyes she most dreaded were filled with tears, stole away to hide her burning blushes in some retired corner. Twenty years afterwards, when she mentioned the little incident, as one of exceeding painfulness at the time of its occurrence, she said nothing, probably she knew nothing, of the murmur of applause which went around the circle, while her own cheeks were tingling with mortification.

It had at first been the intention of young Boardman to accompany Mrs. Judson on her return voyage; but it was afterwards thought advisable for him to remain a little longer at his studies. Beside, a previous appointment had been made by the Board of Missions; and, with Mr. and Mrs. Wade, Mrs. Judson re-traversed intervening oceans, and in the autumn of 1823, joined her husband at Rangoon. A few days found them on their way to Ava. And here the elegant woman, who, but a little while before, had been received in London as an "angel-visitant," shone a brilliant star in the most refined and intellectual circles of Edinboro', and moved the idol of tender hearts and admiring eyes in her own America, was obliged to pass two weeks in a little native boat, moored on the shore; for they had, in her own words, "no home, no house to shelter us from the burning sun by day, and the cold dews by night."

A warning cloud seemed to be settling over the golden city;

there was a strange fluttering in the pulse of power;—but what interest had a mere teacher of religion in these things? How should they interfere with his pursuits? Surely, with the influence which he had gained at court, and his repeated assurances that he was *not* an Englishman, he would be allowed to remain unmolested. So the missionary erected his board cottage, and meekly and patiently, the two sat down to their toilsome labor. But an unexpected voice came up from Bengal—the roar of cannon, and the clash of arms—and, instantly, the royal city seemed as though swarming with banditti.

"They are spies! they are spies!" and lo! at once the cord and the death-prison! Then followed clanking chains and the torturing stocks; then wailed the feeble infant, a strange, lovely guest in such a fearful scene; then the fever raged in the father's veins, and burned upon his brain; and the big tear rolled from fond, beautiful eyes, as the delicate wife and mother crouched before dusky forms, and raised the petitioning voice to hardened ears; and, still, wanton cruelty, cupidity, suspicion, and mocking malice kept up the torture. Still the heavy fetters, pair on pair, bound down the scarred and aching limbs; and still the worst of criminals, thieves, and murderers, were the jailors of Christian men, and jeered on them in the low, disgusting mirth of base, as well as savage natures. So day after day, week after week, and month after month, dragged their weary, weary, rounds, and no change came. None? Ah! the torturing march, beneath a blazing tropic sun at noonday, with blistering flesh, bleeding feet, fainting limbs, and reeling figure, when death came to the prisoners' ranks, and released one poor wretch from his sufferings—this was indeed a change! Then came the terrible shock to the agonized wife, left without a clue in that great horror-haunted city—the anguish of suspense, the hurried search, the savage repulse, the fearful whispers which clothed threatened death with terrible, nameless horrors; and then the infectious malady—disease in various forms, with not one remedy at hand—all these came on with overwhelming power, till even *her* indomitable spirit had well nigh fainted, but that from the prison and the chains came a voice of encouragement, all languid as it was with pain and suffering; and that both hearts leaned confidingly on Heaven. And thus, for the greater part of two long, dragging years, did the benefactors of poor Burmah walk through sufferings far worse than death, while the Christian world were striving in vain to guess their fate.

Meantime, Boardman, with his fair young wife, had embarked for the scene of their future hopes, fears, and toils. Letters dated nearly a year previous, had brought intelligence of hostilities between Burmah and the Bengal government, and of the narrow escape of Messrs. Hough and Wade at Rangoon; but it was known that the English arms were victorious, and there could be little doubt but permanent peace was by this time restored. At least, Rangoon had been seized by the English, and there a home awaited the missionary strangers.

"Beyond the town's remotest confine hid
By thick embowering trees from distant ken,
Where wild beasts in the evening prowled amid
The near dark jungle; and yet wilder men
Nightly marauded; solitary stood
The Mission-House; table, and chair, and mat,
Its furniture, of fashioning most rude;
And close beside it, rose the white zayat,
Beneath whose roof of leaves, all day the teacher sat."

Thither it was their intention to proceed at once, and commence their life labors. Under these impressions, it is a little singular that Mrs. Boardman, when almost in sight of port, should have penned the following words: "Perhaps on our arrival at Calcutta, we shall be informed that Rangoon is regained by the Burmese, and the station abandoned! Perhaps the missionaries at Ava have fallen victims to the implacable vengeance of a people, whose 'tender mercies are cruel.' Or if we should be allowed to settle quietly in Burmah, who knows but some unforeseen revolution may occasion our expulsion, and we be doomed to rove from shore to shore? You recollect that our first American missionaries were called to endure trials similar to these. It is not impossible that some tree of Central Africa may yet shelter our moldering dust; or the deep, desolating snows of Siberia descend upon the graves of those, who left their homes expecting to labor and die upon the soil of Burmah. We may even fall martyrs to the cause of our precious Saviour. But, my dear Charlotte, it matters little where this poor dust mingles with its kindred dust, if but the spirit be prepared to ascend to regions of eternal blessedness. My whole desire is to live devoted to God on earth; and, when the hour of dissolution comes, let me behold Jesus smiling upon me, and I shall be happy, even though amid tortures and flames."

The next letter is filled with sorrowful tidings, for all missionary labor was suspended in Burmah; and she adds, "We are exceedingly distressed when we try to picture the fate of our friends at Ava." Under these circumstances, Boardman's only course was to remain in Calcutta until the close of the war, and endeavor to make some preparation for future usefulness. At first he took up his residence in a suburban village, and subsequently in town. Here they were comparatively well situated for study, and lost no time in obtaining a Burmese teacher.

A letter, bearing date April 13, 1826, thus commences: "Rejoice with me, my beloved sister, at the wonderful preservation and deliverance of our dear friends, who for so long a time endured imprisonment, and sufferings innumerable at Ava! The intelligence of their safety has filled our hearts with joy; and has excited within us warm emotions of gratitude to that beneficent Being, who never leaves nor forsakes those who put their trust in Him. Doct. and Mrs. Judson are now in Rangoon, and Doct. Price is with us, in Calcutta."

Rangoon had been, by the treaty, restored to the Burmese, and it now became the first business of the missionaries to find some spot under the British government, where the wandering dove of gospel peace might find some little rest for the sole of her foot. In relation to this Mr. Boardman says: "Mr. Judson wrote us not long since, that he was just going in company with Commissioner Crawford to explore and survey a tract of land, lying on the Martaban River, where the English propose to erect a town, to be the emporium of their trade with Burmah. Should a town be erected under favorable prospects, it seems probable that it may become the seat of our prominent missionary establishment."

Amherst was at last decided upon as the seat of the new station; and Mr. and Mrs. Wade immediately proceeded thither from Calcutta. But before they reached it, Ann H. Judson had laid her martyr-head beneath the Hopia, crowning the green mound which overlooks the ocean. Death had made an early visit; and there was yet a puny, wailing infant, who but waited the same call. The new station was established in lowliness of spirit, in humility, in sorrowing, and tears.

In compliance with a pressing invitation from the Circular Road church, and with the advice of the other missionaries, Mr. Boardman remained several months longer at Calcutta, until some plan of operation might be so far matured, as to require his labors in Burmah. Under date of January, 1827, Mrs. Boardman thus writes to a friend: "I sometimes think, that of all God's creatures, I have most occasion for gratitude. Since I bade adieu to my native land, the events that have transpired in relation to me have been one series of mercies. I am blest with excellent health, a most affectionate husband, a lovely daughter, and everything in my outward circumstances to make me comfortable and happy. In view of these temporal mercies, I can indeed say, my cup runneth over! But when I think of my spiritual privileges, I am still more overwhelmed. Among these, the near prospect of being actually engaged in the glorious cause of missions, is by no means the least. I still feel it to be a privilege of which I am utterly unworthy, but for which, I hope, I am not altogether unthankful."

Yet, notwithstanding passages like the above, Mrs. Boardman's after testimony proves that her residence in Calcutta did not conduce to her spirituality in religion. Whatever might have been her improvement in other respects, she did not make that progress in the wisdom which is foolishness to the men of this world, those advances in the grace of Christ, which her previous course had promised. Delay had brushed the first bloom from her enthusiasm, and though it might give place to something better and more enduring, which was to come hereafter, the present effect was to be regretted. She was a lovely wife, a fond, proud mother, a most attractive companion, and an accomplished lady. It has been written of her that her English friends, at this time, regarded her "as the most finished and faultless specimen of an American woman that they had ever known." She was a Christian, too, preferring in her heart of hearts the service of her blessed Saviour, to any pleasures or distinctions that the world can give; but her position was not favorable to the development of fervent, heart-piety. Worldly prosperity, and idleness, (a kind of spiritual-idleness, I mean; for Mrs. Boardman's hands and head were doubtless busy) are great enemies to growth in grace, and both of these were incidental to her position. She was not yet on her own missionary ground, and the people, to whom her heart had gone, were not about her; so, while Mr. Boardman, in his less limited capacity of a preacher and a man, could say, "I never had so much reason to believe that God was with me, to bless my labors, as I have had here," she was only studying a dry, difficult language, and looking to the future for usefulness. Her love to God, though real, at times fervent, and always sufficiently strong to render her capable of any sacrifice of worldly advantage to duty, had not yet been ripened by long exercise, nor chastened by sorrow. The news of the death of a little brother, for whom she had felt the half-maternal tenderness natural to an elder sister, startled her, for a moment, from a state of spiritual lukewarmness. Pathetic were the appeals made to her other brothers and her sisters, for preparation to meet the lost little one; and pointed and emphatic were her heart-questions. Indeed, constant warnings to the family friends, from whom she had parted, were never neglected from the time she looked her last upon them in the land of her birth, till her failing hand dropped the pen for ever. The following is a part of a poem, written after the bereavement above mentioned:

"Oh, I remember well the time when thou,
A little child, first lisped thy evening prayer.
Then I was wont to kneel beside thy cot,
And plead for blessings on thine infant head;
And when I'd kissed thy cheek, and wished for thee
A night of pleasant sleep and joyful morn,
How oft upon my ear thine accents fell,
Plaintive and sweet as is the voice of birds,—
'Come back, dear sister, for a moment come,
And tell me more of that dear Saviour's love;
Teach me to shun the dark and dreadful world,
Where wicked spirits dwell in guilt and shame;
And talk to me of heaven, where Jesus is!'
And often now, in fancy, do I see
Thee on thy bed of languishing and death.
I see thee stretch thy weak and wasted arms,
To clasp thine infant sister; hear thee say,
'Dear mother, give the baby Sarah's name;'
I see thee raise thy glazing eye to heaven,
And hear thee lisp thy simple, dying prayer.
But oh! 'tis fancy all; I was not there,
To hear the gentle pleadings of thy voice,
To smooth thy dying pillow, and to claim
Thy last fond look of love. I was not there,
To soothe thy father's grief, and wipe the tear
From the mild eye of her who gave us birth.
Alas, in sorrow's hour, they looked in vain
For me, their eldest born; but still I know
They were not all alone. Jesus was there;

Upon his breast my brother leaned his head;
His blessed presence softened every grief;
My parents wept, but his kind, soothing hand
Wiped from their eyes the tear, *and all was well.*"

Chapter 5

MAULMAIN

Broad leaves spreading, creepers trailing,
Cast strange, fitful shadows there;
Brilliant blossoms, fruits ne'er failing,
Crimson clouds in azure sailing,
Lade with wealth the slumberous air.

But the hooded serpent's creeping
Where the richest blossoms fall,
From his lair the tiger's leaping;
And dark forms, at midnight creeping,
Ghost-like, glide along the wall.

On the 17th of April, 1827, the Boardmans arrived at Amherst; and in two days after Mrs. Boardman was first attacked by the disease which made her an invalid for many years; and which, finally, after a long interval of health, brought her to the grave. How peculiarly saddening must any illness have seemed at this crisis; when, after an absence of nearly two years from her native land, she had just set foot, for the first time, upon the soil of Burmah. Her little daughter, also, the beautiful, rosy-cheeked Sarah, of whom she had so often spoken in her letters, with the proud fondness of a young mother, was even more a sufferer than she. And they had come to no place of joy. The shadowy form of the great Destroyer had scarce passed from the door of the rude mission-house; but yet he turned back, and stood again upon the threshold. Almost the first labor of Mr. Boardman's hands was to construct the small, last house, "doorless and dark within," of a little being, (the infant first pillowed among her father's chains at Ava) who might tell her sister seraphs of a short life still darker. He assisted in laying Maria Judson by her mother's side, and then walked beside the one sorely-stricken mourner, back to his own family of invalids.

It was soon resolved that the three missionaries should attempt the occupation of both Amherst and Maulmain, twenty-five miles apart; and the Boardmans immediately prepared for removal. A small bamboo house, a very frail shelter in the eyes of an American, was erected for them at Maulmain as soon as practicable; and Mrs. Boardman was carried to the water-side upon a litter, to be placed in the boat which was to convey her to her new home. A row of native houses had sprung up along the river-side, and the little town was daily receiving accessions to its population, from those who preferred the English government to their own. The Mission-House was in a lonely spot, about a mile from the cantonments, and the thick jungle close at hand, was the haunt of wild beasts, whose howlings sounded dismally on their ears in the night-time. Behind them rose a handsome range of hills, tipped here and there with the mark of a nation's idolatry—the light, graceful pagoda, with its white or gilded masonry, and glittering ornaments; and before them rolled a broad, beautiful river, in which an English sloop of war was lying at anchor, and curiously-shaped Indian boats were passing to and fro, with each changing tide. Just across the river, lay the Burman province of Martaban, which having been deserted by its peaceful inhabitants, became, to the terrible men who took shelter there, like his own mountain-fastnesses to MacGregor. Armed with knives, spears, and sometimes muskets, they sallied forth in parties of twenty or thirty, at nightfall; and then woe to the poor wretch who was suspected of having treasure worth the trouble of a visit.

Sometimes even entire villages were destroyed by them, and they once ventured so far as to attack a guard of sepoys. Stealthily they moved, with a tread as light as the Indians of the western world; and when they had secured their booty, the Martaban coast became to them the altar of Jupiter. By touching that, they were safe, for it was beyond the jurisdiction of the English; and so they carried on their daring trade with impunity. The English general had suggested to Mr. Boardman that he might be exposing himself to danger, both from these lawless men and the wild beasts of the jungle; and had invited him to take up his residence within the cantonments. But this would have defeated the missionary's object; for to serve the Burmese, or even prepare to serve them, by studying their character and language, he must be with them.

Here, in a place well-calculated, from its loneliness, for study, Mrs. Boardman applied herself to the acquisition of the language very successfully; for she had the advantage of hearing it spoken daily. She even attempted to converse with the half-wild children, who stood gaping at her in amused curiosity; and attracted them about her as much as possible, in the hope that, as soon as she was prepared, she might be able to establish a school. "Oh! for a common language!" has been the half-impatient exclamation of many in her situation. To the eyes of purblind mortals, it seems a great pity that the curse of Babel could not have been restricted to those who make themselves strong only to do evil.

About a month after Mrs. Boardman's arrival at Maulmain, under date of June 20th, she writes a friend: "We are in excellent health, and as happy as it is possible for human beings to be upon earth. It is our earnest desire to live, and labor, and die, among this people."

Four days passed after the writing of this letter, as previous ones had passed; men in loose garments of gayly-plaided cloth, and with their long, black hair wound about their heads, and confined by folds of muslin, looked curiously in at the door of the strange foreigner; and then encouraged by some kind word or glance, or the spreading of a mat, seated themselves in their own fashion, talked a little while with their host, though often, from misapprehension of each other's meaning, at cross-purposes, and went away, leaving him to his books and teacher. Women and children gathered more timidly, but with curiosity even less disguised, about the *Kalah-ma-pyoo*, (white foreigness) wondering at her strange costume, the fairness of her skin, and the superiority displayed in her bearing; and some of the bolder of them venturing to touch her hand, or to pass their tawny, taper fingers from the covered instep to the toe of the neatly-formed slipper, so unlike their own clumsy sandals. But who, among all these, came to inquire of Jesus Christ, or learn the way to heaven? Most emphatically could they say, "We have not so much as heard if there be a God."

On the evening of the fourth day, as it deepened into night, the books of study were thrown aside, and the book of God taken in their stead; then the prayer was raised to heaven, and the little family went to rest. Feeble were the rays of the one pale lamp, close by the pillow of the young mother, scarce throwing its light upon the infant resting in her bosom, and penetrating into the remote darkness, but by feeble flickerings. So sleep soon brooded over the shut eyelids; and silence folded its solemn wings about the little habitation.

The infant stirred, and the mother opened her eyes. Why was she in darkness? and what objects were those scattered so strangely about her apartment, just distinguishable from the gray shadows? The lamp was soon relighted, and startling was the scene which it revealed. There lay, in odd confusion, trunks, boxes, and chests of drawers, all rifled of their contents; and strewed carelessly about the floor, were such articles as the marauders had not considered worth their taking. While regarding in consternation, not appreciable by those who have access to the shops of an American city, this spoiling of their goods, Mrs. Boardman chanced to raise her eye to the curtain, beneath which her husband had slept, and she thought of the lost goods no more. Two long gashes, one at the head and the other at the foot, had been cut in the muslin; and there had the desperate villains stood, glaring on the unconscious sleeper with their fierce, murderous eyes, while the booty was secured by their companions. The bared, swarthy arm was ready for the blow, and the sharp knife or pointed spear glittered in their hands. Had the sleeper opened his eyes, had he only stirred, had but a heavy, long-drawn breath startled the cowardice of guilt—ah, had it! But it did not. The rounded limbs of the little infant lay motionless as their marble counterfeit; for if the rosy lips had moved but to the slightest murmur, or the tiny hand crept closer to the loved bosom in her baby dreams, the chord in the mother's breast must have answered, and the death-stroke followed. But the mother held her treasure to her heart and slept on. Murderers stood by the bedside, regarding with callous hearts, the beautiful tableau; and the husband and father *slept*. But there was one Eye open—the Eye that never slumbers; a protecting wing was over them, and a soft, invisible hand pressed down their sleeping lids.

Nearly every article of value, that could be taken away, had disappeared from the house; and though strict search was made throughout the neighborhood, no trace of them was ever discovered. After this incident, Sir Archibald Campbell furnished the house with a guard of Sepoys during the night; and as the rapid increase of the population soon gave it a central position in the town, the danger of such attacks was very much lessened.

In a simple, child-like letter to a little sister, dated December of the same year, Mrs. Boardman writes: "I have a Sabbath-School of little Burman girls, who are learning their catechism and their prayers. We have no hymns in the Burmese, or I should teach them hymns also. We have, beside this, a school during the week," (Mrs. Wade's school, mostly from Amherst) "in which the tawny little girls learn to read and sew. They are also learning the multiplication table; and they are just beginning the first part of the same arithmetic which you study, translated into the language. These poor little girls would have nobody to tell them of God and of Christ, of heaven and of hell, if there were no missionaries here. Are you not glad that your sister Sarah has come to tell them of these important things?"

In January she announces, with earnest warmth of language, the first baptism she had looked upon in Burmah—two native converts, by the senior missionary. She adds, "there is also one more person, a Karen, who will probably soon be baptized. He is a poor man, and has been for some time past in the employ of Doct. Judson." Probably she did not know that this poor man had formerly been one of the most desperate of his race, a robber and a murderer; and, certainly, she could not foresee to what honor God had reserved him. This singular man, whose first ideas of the Christian religion were gleaned from a tract presented him at Rangoon, was the famous Ko Thah-Byoo; whose rough and undisciplined genius, energy and zeal, have won for him an enviable reputation, as one of the boldest pioneers in the Karen mission. He was, soon after this mention in the letter, examined and approved by the Maulmain church; and was baptized by Mr. Boardman on his first arrival at Tavoy.

Perhaps something ought to be said of the general character of Mrs. Boardman's letters, if for no other reason, as an excuse for less copious extracts than we could wish, and for these being usually in fragments. She says but little in them of herself—her doings and feelings; but she seems full of interest in those she addresses, sympathizing in their minutest concerns, with that unselfish kindness which is sweet to the recipient, though to a stranger uninteresting. They must have been delicious indeed to those she loved; but, like some of the most important passages in every human life, they are not fitted for the public eye.

I have unfolded a letter, since finishing the above sentence, in which every member of her father's large family is thanked by name for having written her; and each allusion is accompanied by some affectionate comment, or word of praise or encouragement, suited to the age of her young correspondent. At last she says, "You must let the dear little twins and my sweet sister, whom I have not seen, *make each a mark upon a paper*, that I may have some token from their little hands." There is something exceedingly touching in the affectionate simplicity of this request, which will not fail to find its way to many a heart.

It has been said of Mrs. Boardman, (though referring to a much later period of her life) that she excelled in the maternal relation. With her letters before me, and the various anecdotes gathered from different sources, fresh in memory, I cannot but conclude that she excelled in all domestic relations. The tender devotedness of the daughter, the affectionate, sympathetic faithfulness of the sister, (to say nothing of a tie yet stronger and holier) were only different developments of the same character, which was perfected in the mother. The following fragment, showing how her thoughts still turned homeward, though she says that the "wide world would not induce her to return," is from a letter written to her parents on the third anniversary of their parting day. We give but a few of the opening lines.

"I see the dear parental dwelling-place,
Where love and happiness were constant guests;
I see my aged grandsire, seated near
That good old pilgrim who has been his joy,
Through many years of hope, and care, and pain;
I see my dear, kind parents, side by side,
Smiling with pleased affection on the group
Of children sporting round the cheerful hearth;
Oh, *I* was once of that most happy group!"

Chapter 6

TAVOY

"Light for the darkened earth!
Ye blessed, its beams who shed!
Shrink not till the day-spring hath its birth,
Till, wherever the footstep of man doth tread
Salvation's banner spread widely forth,
Shall gild the dream of the cradle-bed,
And clear the tomb
From its lingering gloom,
For the aged to rest his weary head."

—*Mrs. Sigourney.*

It was at Tavoy, whither he repaired in the spring of 1828, that Mr. Boardman's missionary career really commenced. During their residence at Calcutta, they had studied the language to great disadvantage; and it required all the interval between their arrival at Amherst, and final settlement at Tavoy, to learn to frame even simple sentences, after a model so entirely new to them. Then there were the organs of speech to be disciplined to the utterance of uncouth sounds never heard before, and in which the slightest variation of tone or the change of a letter, so alters the meaning of the word, that the whole sentence is rendered unintelligible.[1] Persons in

1 A somewhat ludicrous mistake of this nature fell under my observation not long since. An English gentleman, who had resided but a short time in Burmah,

America spend many years over languages closely analogous to our own, and then speak and write them with difficulty. The acquisition of an Asiatic language is a vastly more difficult thing; but many persons seem to suppose that the modern missionary has received the miraculous gift of tongues; for they begin to look for "interesting accounts," long before he can possibly be qualified to judge between an inquirer and the most open impostor, who smiles assent to sentiments he does not understand, while he thinks he sees in prospective the *anna*, which is to purchase tomorrow's food.

The Boardmans were met with another difficulty at Tavoy; for the corrupt dialect of the Tavoyans differed from the pure Burmese, more widely than the worst of Canadian Patois from the flowing language of the French capital; and the women, more especially, could not be made to comprehend a sentence without a provincial interpreter. Mr. Boardman's first work after his arrival was to baptize Ko Thah-Byoo, the zealous Karen disciple already mentioned, and the next—but we will quote from Mrs. Boardman's letter to her sister: "My dear husband has just been repairing an old zayat, where he intends to spend a part of each day in recommending the religion of our blessed Saviour to all who will listen. He enters upon public labors with fear and trembling; and I am assured that he has hope in God, and in Him only. He has Burmese worship with the boys of the school," (four boys who accompanied him from Maulmain) "and the two native assistants, every evening, and also divine service each Lord's day morning." What with all health, necessary study, and the care of a family, increased by the boys of the boarding-school, it could not reasonably be expected that Mrs. Boardman would find much time for other duties. She, however, in the words

---

remarked that he had learned two phrases—the one "go," (in the imperative) and the other "make haste;" the first, he said, was always comprehended without difficulty; but the other, (smiling as he spoke, at the characteristic indolence of the people) was never understood—they only turned around and stared vacantly in his face. "What do you say for 'make haste?'" inquired a listener. *"Myeen! myeen!"* was the ready reply. He had changed the *a* to *ee*, and so, when he wished to hasten the movements of his servants, he called out, *"Horse! horse!"*

of her husband, after "Unwearied toil, repeated repulses, and discouragements," succeeded in establishing a girls' school; and as soon as possible employed a woman, whom she had herself taught to read, as an assistant. She thus speaks of a visit to this school: "I am just returned from one of the day-schools. The sun had not risen when I arrived, but the little girls were in the house ready for instruction. My walk to this school is through a retired road, shaded on one side by the old wall of the city, which is overgrown by wild creepers and pole-flowers, and on the other by large fruit-trees. While going and returning, I find it sweet and profitable to think on the shortness of time, the vanity of this delusive world—and oh! I have had some precious views of that world where the 'weary are at rest;' and where sin, that enemy of God, and now constant disturber of my peace, will no more afflict me."

The following quotation from another letter, will give us a glimpse of the state of things a few months later. She describes her own station, by her table, in a little back verandah, and then goes on with her picture thus: "In the room before me sits my dear husband, surrounded by nine little heathen boys, to whom he is imparting a knowledge of that gospel, which can save from eternal ruin. On each side of the house is a long verandah. In one of these the native Christians are holding a prayer-meeting in Burmese, and in the other sits the Chinese convert, Kee Zea-Chung, loudly urging three or four of his deluded countrymen to turn from the worship of idols to that of the true God."

In February, 1829, Mr. Boardman made his first tour among the Karens; leaving his wife, who had but just recovered from an illness of four months' duration, with her two little ones, (the younger a son six months of age) and the boys' boarding-school. She is thus consoled by a Karen woman, the wife of Ko Thah-Byoo: "Weep not, mama; the teacher has gone on a message of compassion to my poor, perishing countrymen. They have never heard of the true God, and the love of his son Jesus-Christ—Christ, who died upon the cross to save sinners. They know nothing of the true religion, mama; and when they die, they cannot go to the golden country of the blessed. God will take care of the teacher; do not weep, mama."

It may seem a weakness to weep an absence, which is to be only of two or three weeks' duration; but one of the beauties of true Christian heroism is the softness which it always leaves upon the spirit. "I should have no objection to seeing the woman I loved a devout believer in these things," said an infidel to me once in a public stage-coach; "for there is something in them which subdues the character, and produces a kind of tearful and yet elevated tenderness, not to be lightly esteemed in a cold, selfish world like this. I speak from experience, for my wife is a Christian." But partings among missionaries, where one goes to endure privations and toils in an unexplored jungle, and the other is left without a protector in the midst of a large, idolatrous city, are sadly unlike the same thing on Christian soil. The consecration of the missionary, adds iron to neither heart nor nerve. This is the same delicate woman whom you would have hesitated to leave alone in a civilized land, though friends might have been within call from your very door—who would not have walked the streets of a civilized city at nightfall without a protector. And what new armor has she now, that she should stand, perhaps thronged by innumerable trials, with dusky faces about her, and strange voices sounding in her ears; and not a lip to whisper, in the accents of her native tongue, one single word of encouragement and sympathy? True, she may be left with a little band of disciples, but with them she has only one theme in common—the salvation of Jesus Christ—and even in that knowledge they are mere infants. The high religious truths which she loves to contemplate, are entirely beyond their grasp. Her refinement, her sensitiveness, all the higher emotions of heart and soul, are even farther from their comprehension than her superiority of intellect and systematic mental culture. Even her horror of crime, the black deeds which defile the very atmosphere she breathes, they cannot appreciate; for, with the partially-cleared vision of a weak, ignorant, faltering disciple, they yet see everything through the medium of confirmed habit. What their fathers and grandfathers did, and what they have done unblushingly from childhood, loses its blackness in their eyes, although they know it to be sin. Then, if sickness come, or any new sorrow—oh! there is scarce a person on earth so utterly desolate as the missionary's wife, left alone with her cares—but for the God above her and in her heart.

It would be irrelevant to follow Mr. Boardman, in his trackless march through the Karen wilderness, however interesting must be such a journey. Over hills, and across streams, and ravines almost impassable, he went; the fierce, wily tiger, crouching among the rocks, and mischievous fairy Pucks, in the shape of grinning, chattering monkeys, swinging from the boughs overhead; huge mountains stretching far into the clouds, with the wild streamlets, which fed some mighty river, dashing, bounding and leaping from rock to rock, down their precipitous sides, like snow-wreaths gifted with the spirit of life; and, far down in the deep valley, the calm Palouk, rolling slowly and gracefully to its destination, like the river of the good man's life, gliding through its earthly vale to the ocean of a blessed eternity. Among scenes like these, and others wilder and darker, he went, scattering pearls of priceless value in his way, greeting many a thirsty lip with the waters of life, and waking in the dead spirits of the wilderness, a pulse which never beat there before. After two or three weeks he returned, to endure one of the severest trials of the missionary's life. The poison of sin, which had once required the cauterizing knife, previous to the commencement of this tour, again made its appearance in his little church; and his sensitive spirit was wrung with the bitterest anguish. Extreme sensitiveness, and distrust of self were, doubtless, the occasion of much of the sorrow felt both by Mr. and Mrs. Boardman. It was not merely that the cause of Christ had been disgraced through the defection of its supposed friends, but they feared that the disgrace had been somehow occasioned by their own unworthiness or inefficiency. Mrs. Boardman, in particular, was roused and alarmed. From the commencement of her residence in Calcutta, up to the present time, her capacity for religious enjoyment had been but little enlarged, and her attainments in spirituality were of no high order. Still, her self-accusations, though sincere, could not have been deserved. Something of the acuteness of her feelings may be learned from a letter to Mrs. Bolles. It is full of the bitterest self-upbraidings, and there is a spirit of the deepest humiliation breathing in every line.

"Some of these poor Burmans," she says, "who are daily carried to the grave, may at last reproach me, and say, 'you came, it is true, to the city where we dwelt, to tell of heaven and hell, but wasted much, much of your precious time in indolence, while acquiring our language. And, when you were able to speak, why were you not *incessantly* telling us of this day of doom, when we visited you why, oh why did you ever speak of any other thing while we were ignorant of the most momentous of all truths? Oh! how could you think on anything but our salvation? How could you sleep, or allow yourself anything like ease or comfort, while we were perishing, and you knew a Being who could save us, and that Being had promised to grant the petition of his children? You told us that He was your Father, that He heard your lowest whispers and most secret sighs—why, then, did you not, day and night, entreat Him in our behalf?'

"Mr. Boardman will tell you of the heart-rending afflictions which we have been called to endure in our little church. Our hearts have almost bled with anguish, and mine has sunk lower than the grave, for I have felt that my unworthiness has been the cause of all our calamities."

This trial, which only one class of readers, (*heart*-Christians) will be able to appreciate, ended in a blessing; for from this time, the things of heaven began to gain a stronger and firmer hold upon her heart, and a domestic calamity, which soon followed, gave, even while its shadow lay heaviest, additional value to the blessing.

In the spring of 1829, Mrs. Boardman was again visited by severe illness, and her physical constitution became so much impaired, that she was unable to rally, as on former occasions. Her infant son, too, was a pale, puny creature, with his father's spiritual look—the same delicate fashioning of feature and transparency of complexion, and the same blue veins crossing the temples. And the father was not quite like his former self. His cheeks were a little more hollow, and the color on them more flickering; his eyes were brighter, and seemingly more deeply set beneath the brow, and immediately below them was a faint, indistinct arc of mingled ash and purple, like the shadow of a fading leaf; his lips were sometimes of a clayey pallor, and sometimes they glowed with crimson; and his fingers were long, and the hands of a partially transparent thinness. None of the family were in health, except the "rosy little daughter,"— the "bright, beautiful darling Sarah Ann," as she was fondly named in many a letter; and she was their joy and pride. A short trip to Mergui, sea-air and sea-bathing proved beneficial to them, however and they returned to their toil with renewed strength and vigor.

Chapter 7

LITTLE SARAH

"He gazed at the flowers with tearful eyes,
He kissed their drooping leaves;
It was for the Lord of Paradise,
He bound them in his sheaves.

'My Lord has need of these flowerets gay,'
The Reaper said, and smiled;
Dear tokens of the earth are they,
Where he was once a child."

—*Longfellow.*

Sarah is as plump and rosy-cheeked as we could wish. Oh! how delighted you would be to see her, and hear her prattle! Thus wrote the mother in her happiness; and, in a little more than two weeks after, she saw her darling, speechless and motionless, in her little shroud. "I knew all the time," says the bereaved parent, "that she was very ill; but it did not once occur to me that she might die, till she was seized with the apoplexy, about three hours before she closed her eyes upon us for ever. Oh! the agony of that moment!" And in that agonized moment, as the shadow of eternity fell upon the spirit of the little sufferer, and a vista, which her eye could not discern, but from which her failing nature instinctively recoiled, opened before her, she looked with anxious alarm into her mother's face, and exclaimed:—"I frightened! mama! I frightened!" What a strange thing is death. The tender nursling, who in moments of even imagined ill, had clung to the mother's bosom, and been sheltered in her arms, now hovered over a dark, unfathomed gulf, and turned pleadingly to the same shield—but it had failed. The mother's arm was powerless; her foot could not follow; and the trembling babe passed on alone, to find her fears allayed on an angel's bosom. Mrs. Boardman followed her first-born to the grave with faltering steps, and then returned to her other stricken child. "He lay," she says, "feeble and emaciated, in the arms of his nurse; and, for the first time since he was two months old, refused to notice us. On the next Sabbath night, we watched him till morning, expecting every breath to be his last. But our Heavenly Father is kind, and he did not take from us both our blossoms." The following remembrances, penned nearly a year after the sorrowful bereavement, are for the eye of mothers, whose thoughts turn often to a little grave, and then back to the bounding life and infantine endearments, which preceded its solemn stillness.

"Our little Sarah left us July 8th, of last year—aged two years and eight months. . . . She was a singularly lovely child. Her bright blue eyes, yellow hair, and rosy cheeks, formed a striking contrast to the little dark faces around her; and I often said—

Thou art a sweet and fragrant flower,
'Mid poisonous, vile weeds blooming;
A lovely star, whose cheering power
Makes glad the heavy-footed hour,
When midnight clouds are glooming.

From the time she began to notice anything, we were the objects of her fondest love. If she thought she had incurred our displeasure, her tender heart seemed ready to burst; and she could not rest for a moment, until she had said she was 'sorry,' and obtained the kiss of forgiveness. She had learned to obey us implicitly. . . . Always when she saw us kneeling to pray, she would come and kneel beside us. On observing me one day going to a small house for prayer, near the spot where her precious dust now sleeps, she said to Marian and Rosina, 'Go back! I will go alone with mama to pray!' She followed me to the place, and as soon as she entered it, threw herself on her knees and commenced praying.

She was an exceedingly sensitive child. She was not only afflicted at sight of our tears, but even a sorrowful look from us melted her tender heart, and incited her to do all in her power to alleviate our sorrows. If we frowned upon her conduct she wept, kissed us, and refrained from committing the same fault again. If either of us was ill, her heart seemed overflowing with grief; and she would say, in tones of touching tenderness, 'Mama,' (or papa) 'ill—Sarah very sad. Mama cannot take Sarah now.' And she would come and stroke our foreheads with her little soft hand, and kiss us *so* affectionately! Her love to her little brother George was unlimited. From the day of his birth till the day but one before she died, he was her idol. If she wanted anything ever so much, only tell her it was for Georgie, and that was enough to satisfy her. She never envied him an article of dress or food, or a plaything, but would always resign her choicest toys to her dear little brother. Three days before she died, she was lying uneasily in a large swing cradle, and George was in the same room, crying. We thought it might soothe the little sufferer, for he was also very ill, to lay him down beside Sarah. The proposal delighted her; with smiles she threw open her little arms, and, for the last time, held her darling brother in her fond embrace. So great was her gratification at this privilege, that she seemed to forget her own pains.

Little Sarah spoke English remarkably well for so young a child, and Burmese, like a native; she could also say some things in the Hindostanee and Karen. And what seems a little singular, she never confounded two languages, but always spoke pure English to us, and pure Burmese to Burmans. This discrimination continued as long as she had the powers of speech. She had learned the Lord's prayer and several little hymns. Dr. Judson's lines on the death of Mee-Shway-ee she knew by heart in Burmese, and used to chant them for half an hour at a time. She had nearly learned the Burman and English alphabets, and could repeat the names of the months, days of the week, and a part of the multiplication-table, in Burmese. These things may seem very trivial to you, but I muse upon them by the hour together; and it is only when I call my cooler judgment into action, that I can make myself believe they are uninteresting to any person on earth. I love to think of my sweet bud of immortality, expanding so beautifully in my own presence; and fancy I can judge, in some small degree, of the brilliancy of the perfect flower, from these little developments.

A few hours before she died, she called us to her, kissed us, and passed her dear hand, still full and dimpled, as in health, softly over our faces. The pupils of her eye were so dilated that she could not see us distinctly, and once, for a moment or two, her mind seemed to be wandering; then looking anxiously into my face, she said, 'I frightened, mama! I frightened!' . . . Oh! with what feelings did I wash and dress her lovely form for the last time, and compose her perfect little limbs; and then see her—the dear child, which had so long lain in my bosom—borne away to her newly-made grave. My heart grew faint when I thought that I had performed for her my last office of love; that she would never need a mother's hand again. My dear husband performed the funeral service with an aching, though not desponding heart. The grave is in our own enclosure, about fifteen rods from the house—a beautiful, retired spot, in a grove of Gangau trees. Near it is a little Bethel, erected for private devotion. Thither we have often repaired; and we trust that God, who in his infinite wisdom has taken our treasure to himself, often meets us there."

"It never once occurred to me," wrote Mrs. Boardman, while seated by the shrouded form of her dead child, (thus opening her oppressed heart to a friend, who had known something of her religious state previous to this), "It never once occurred to me, all the time my child was with me, that she could die; she seemed always so full of life and health." In the depths of grief and lowly penitence, were these words penned, for the stricken mourner attempted no excuse. She hesitated not to acknowledge, that it was a strange, an almost incredible forgetfulness, and that her bereavement, bitter as it was, was a reminder from heaven, sent, not only in justice, but in mercy; and in tearful, repentant, sorrowing humility, she bowed beneath her Father's rod, grateful for the love which directed the blow, though it descended crushingly upon her spirit. She knew that this affliction was sent to call back her wandering heart to its place the foot of the Cross; and with the confiding submission of a little child, she obeyed the summons.

A single error, which had stolen upon her insensibly, through the speculative conversations of a friend, to whose opinions she yielded much deference, had contributed, in a great degree, to keep her in a state of spiritual darkness. The poison, (for it can be called no less) was imbibed in America, though its workings could not appear, while she was surrounded by Christian friends, and while nothing occurred to wear away her zeal. But during her residence in Calcutta, it had crept into her spirit imperceptibly, and the living principle had been thus deprived of its activity. She had lost the eye of faith, which discerns the finger of the Almighty in the minute concerns of life. She did not believe that the great Jehovah condescends to regard our going-out and our coming-in, our lying-down and our rising-up; that he watches momentarily over our individual good, and marks out our paths in flowery ways, or sharpens the thorns beneath our feet, as He sees will best contribute to that good. She, of course, never doubted a general superintending Providence; but she could not reconcile the vastness of His power, who holds the reins of the universe in His hand, with the minute care, which wings the little bird, feather by feather, counts out human life by pulsations, and maintains a yet tender and more watchful supervision over His own peculiar people. But when the child, on which she doted, was removed from her sight there was something in her heart, which told her by whose hand, and for what purpose, this desolation had been wrought. The worldling would have seen nothing in it but the fulfilling of a universal law of nature; but, by the light that had not been extinguished in her spirit, she read, in the sad characters of the grave, a message to herself. She knew that the omniscient God, whose care had been over her personally, though she had scarce discerned it, through happy years, had planned and wrought this seeming ill for the deepest good. From that moment, her vision was cleared; and she learned to wait, and watch, and obey, as a little child looks to his father's face, and reads his will in smiles or frowns, or in the glances of the eye. And bearing with her, ever after, this sweet trustfulness, she passed through other severer trials, sometimes with weeping eye, but never with a fainting heart. With the monarch-minstrel of Israel, she could say, "Though I walk through the valley of the shadow of death, I will fear no evil; Thy rod and Thy staff, they comfort me."

Of little George, after his recovery, Mrs. Boardman writes: "We have a fine, healthy boy; but I do not allow myself to idolize him, as I did his dear departed sister. In her dissolution, we saw such a wreck of all that was lovely and beautiful, that I think we shall henceforth be kept from worshipping the creature." Well was it, that the mother had placed this guard over her heart, for she had need of it. In the succeeding January, another precious bud was given to her bosom; and, in less than a year after, that, too, was "bound in the sheaf" of the "reaper, death." But previous to this, before little George had lifted his head from his pillow of pain, or a green blade had appeared on Sarah's grave, came events fearfully spirit-stirring; and to these we will now return.

Chapter 8

THE REVOLT

"Ah me! there was a smell of death,
Hung round us night and day."
—*Mary Howitt.*

At the dead hour of night, in the early part of the succeeding month of August, a lad belonging to the boarding-school was awakened by a party of men from the jungle, passing near the house, which was just without the city walls, by the northern gate. It was not a strange incident; but the boy had sufficient curiosity to peep through the crevices in the braided bamboo walls of his sleeping-room, and watch them till they had gained admittance to the town. This party was, from time to time, followed by several others, who talked in low tones of lost buffaloes, of which they seemed to be in search, till the wondering watcher began to believe that all the herds of the jungle must have abjured their leafy homes, in favor of a town residence. It did not escape the lad's notice, that the shadows of the distant trees were strangely like living men, and that little knots of real men were collecting here and there, where there were no shadows, all in busy consultation; and, from time to time, making violent gestures, and pointing towards the gate, through which the buffalo-seekers had passed, and then to the top of the wall, and then—he might be mistaken, but he thought they pointed to the house of his master. His hair began to rise, and his timid heart to flutter, when lo! a fierce yell from a hundred savage voices, answered by a few straggling shots; and he saw, in the gray of coming morning, a thin cloud of black smoke eddying away over the town-wall.

"Dawai tah! Dawai tah!"[1] cried, in the same instant, a voice, which seemed close beside him; "ho-o-o! tsayah, thaken! Dawai tah!" and the frail house jarred with the rattling of doors and windows.

Mr. Boardman had been aroused from a sound sleep, and not comprehending the sudden uproar, threw open his door, and stood upon the threshold, armed for the defense of his family.

"No! no!" again shouted the friendly voice; "you understand not! Tavoy has risen—all the province is in arms! Be quiet, teacher; you can do no good!" Tavoy in rebellion! this was indeed alarming information; for a more defenseless town was never in possession of powerful conquerors. No English troops had been stationed there; and there were only about a hundred sepoys, who, arranged with the most consummate military skill, man by man, could not occupy the entire wall of the long, straggling city. They mounted a few small field-pieces; but the gunner was ill, and the English officer in command of the detachment was known to be on his death-bed. To complete the helplessness of their condition, Col. Burney, who was both military and civil chief, was absent at Maulmain; and the direction of affairs at this terrible crisis devolved on a very young physician, with no adviser but Mrs. Burney.

While Mr. Boardman took this rapid view of the state of the besieged town, the firing and the hideous yells continued with unabated vigor. It was soon ascertained that a party of two hundred men, armed with clubs, knives, spears, and occasionally a musket, had rushed upon the powder-magazine and gun-shed, which were defended by a guard of six sepoys only, and under a native officer. The brave fellows knew that to lose these was to yield the town at once; and they firmly opposed their trained-skill, few as they were, to the ill-regulated force of their numerous assailants. The magazine

1 (Provincial) Tavoy has risen!

was very near the gate, and Mr. Boardman was just beginning to apprehend danger from the flight of the bullets in the direction of his house; when another cause for alarm presented itself. Parties had been gathering beneath the walls from every direction; and now one of these paused close by his own compound, as though for consultation. He saw their dusky visages turned in the direction of his home, their dark eyes gleaming fiercely, as they leaned upon their spears; and their expressive gestures told him that the fate of his little family depended on that moment. He was a peaceful man, but he carried a white face, and wore the costume of the English. His trembling wife caught her pale, emaciated infant to her bosom, and hurried to a low wooden shed, beyond the house, open on the least exposed side. Here she crouched upon the floor, to escape the bullets, which she was told were passing above her; while her husband, with the boy-watcher of the night before, waited the result within. But the party dispersed without attempting harm; and in about an hour the victorious sepoys were in possession of all the city gates. The insurgents were successfully repulsed, and retreated beyond the city walls, leaving sixty slain, and their leader a prisoner. In the meantime, other parties of the rebels had been going about the town, committing various depredations; and a hundred desperate wretches, loosed from the fetters imposed by English justice, sprang from the city prisons with the eagerness of blood-hounds on the scent.

Mr. Boardman seized the moment of quiet, succeeding the repulse of the magazine party, to flee, with his wife and child, to the Government-House; where they were most kindly received by the intrepid lady-commander. The first business of the sepoys was to secure arms and ammunition. Three cannon, and a sufficient quantity of gunpowder, were conveyed to a large wooden building on the wharf; and the remainder of the powder was thrown into wells within the town. This operation, retarded by almost incessant skirmishing, occupied all the time till three o'clock, when the foreigners put themselves in readiness to evacuate the town; for the attempt of a hundred men to hold it against twenty times their number, would have been madness. The Chinese, who had built their shops without the town, along the river side, constituted a party of exclusives, probably fifty in number, professing neutrality; but still they hung upon the skirts of the English, in a manner to insure present safety, and escape any special odium, if the insurrection should, in the end, prove unsuccessful. A few Portuguese traders joined the foreign party, not with the expectation of rendering any assistance, but to gain protection for themselves and families; and one wily old Mussulman, who knew enough of the English to see how the affair must necessarily terminate, seized gladly on what seemed to him a golden opportunity, and lent his aid wherever he could be most serviceable. There were but seven Europeans, beside Mr. Boardman; and Mrs. Burney and Mrs. Boardman were the only ladies. At another time this singular procession, as it passed beyond the gate of the city, must needs have won a smile from an anchorite. The dark line of native soldiers, in their Indian uniform, the mulatto-faced Portuguese, the keen-eyed Mussulman, the long train of women and children, attached to the sepoys and others, stripped of the ornaments which might have roused the cupidity of the enemy, and in the meanest, filthiest apparel, and the handful of English, with their troop of Burmese and Hindoo servants, constituted a singularly motley company. But Mrs. Boardman, as she hurried on her way, now startled from her forced calmness by the hideous yells of the insurgents, or the report of musketry from the defenders of her own party, and again half-springing from her path as her gaze fell upon the glazed, staring eyes and bleeding wounds of the dead beside it, was in no condition to take note of trivial circumstances. One apparition, however, excited her attention, even then—the figure of a man, the very personification of death, as he often comes in an Indian climate, seated on a led horse, at the head of the small detachment. It was the English commander, who had been hurried from his bed to escape the massacre; and who hoped, by appearing in his saddle once more before his men, to give them some little encouragement. But his face was thin and cadaverous, his complexion almost orange in hue, and his eye sunk deeply in its socket; and as Mrs. Boardman looked on his bent, skeleton figure, swaying helplessly to every motion of the animal he bestrode, the sight added a kind of indefinite horror to her impressions of their imminent peril.

The building on the wharf, in which the powder had been deposited, was the retreat chosen; and *such* a retreat! Between three and four hundred persons, with the arms, ammunition, provisions, and necessary baggage for all, huddled together under one roof—persons of different sexes, grades, and nations, forming a disagreeable medley, which it is impossible for one, not conversant with East-Indian scenes, to appreciate. In this company Mrs. Boardman sat down to soothe her pale little sufferer, whose moans of pain now fell more heavily on her aching heart than the sounds of bloodshed without; for how could his failing life be sustained in this terrible place? Beside her, was Mrs. Burney, with her infant son but three weeks old, and these two seemed, in that crowded, miserable place, almost like beings from another world.

Some of the sepoys found shelter within the building, and some in an old shed or two close by; and here for a little time, all breathed more freely. Flying parties of the enemy would now and then attempt an attack, but they were not allowed to come near enough to use their spears, and but little danger was to be apprehended from their muskets. There was time now for cool consultation, and the singular little war-council was conferring together, when a loud report, as of a cannon, turned every visage blank with dismay. A groan broke from the crouching figures that crammed the building, and the boldest and calmest felt their blood pause, and then creep chillingly along its channels.

"They have mounted the cannon, and we are lost!" was the simultaneous exclamation, in various tongues. It had scarce been uttered, before a man stood without the building with a glass at his eye.

"What is it?"

"A jinjal."[1]

"Does it bear upon us?"

"Yes—directly."

A stifled groan—a rustling, rushing sound, as the women threw themselves on their faces, in the oriental style of abandonment to grief—and then a momentary pause.

"What are they doing now?"

"Mounting other pieces—but—but—"

"But what?" impatiently.

"I do not think they will succeed in bringing them within range of us. Ah! they are loading again."

A breathless silence of a few moments succeeded, broken by another report.

"What direction did it take? where did it strike?" were the eager inquiries, while heads were stretched forward with greedy anxiety to catch the answer.

"It passed above us."

"Thank God!" came in an indistinct murmur from a few lips, drowned in exclamations of a different character from the crowd.

"They will aim lower next time."

"Five minutes were passed in the most profound silence, and then another ball sped over the ridge of the thatched roof, and spent itself upon the water."

"They will aim better—they will soon learn."

"Where is the sun?"

"Gone;—not down, but hidden by the trees."

A deep-drawn breath announced the relief which this answer had conveyed; for the long twilights of northern lands are unknown in Burmah, and the firing must needs cease with the darkness which is dense at this season.

Night closed about them at last, though it seemed with unusual slowness; but it brought no cessation of dangers. The stillness was broken by the fierce yells of frequent assailants; and the attempts to

1 A small Burman field-piece.

fire the frail wooden building, made doubly alarming by the presence of gunpowder, were incessant. It was past midnight, when a small boat shot from the black shadows that lay along the shore, dropped silently a few rods farther down the stream, and then crept under the crowded building on the rising tide. The next moment the quick eye of a sepoy detected a sparkle of fire through a crevice in the floor; and stooping lower, and steadying his gaze, till his vision became accustomed to the obscurity, he gained a full view of the figure of the incendiary, in the execution of his terrible design. He raised himself, and applied the muzzle of his musket to the crevice. A scream from those nearest him, (for the act had been too sudden to be understood) and a heavy splash in the water followed the report; and in a few moments, an empty boat was discovered floating away on the surface of the river.

Morning broke upon a weary, half-fainting, dispirited company; and, by its first light, a woman was discovered rocking to and fro, with a dead child upon her knees. It had been suffocated during the accumulated horrors of the night.

At daylight the firing from the walls was renewed, and now the unsuccessful marksman had all day for practice. But it came at long intervals; for the repulse at the magazine had very much weakened the rebels, by depriving them of powder; and that which they manufactured was scarce fit for use. Still the trembling party on the wharf was in imminent danger; for if the piece could once be well-aimed, it would continue to pour an incessant fire upon them, without mercy. Thus passed two more days, and thus passed, in still greater danger, two sleepless nights, till the fifth evening, from the night of the revolt, darkened. This was a terrible night. On three sides of them curled the red flames from burning houses; and just as it rose highest, filling the air with showers of glittering sparkles, a band of five hundred men raised the terrible war-cry, and rushed from the open spaces between the blaze, upon their intended victims. But at that moment a heavy shower of rain descended, and quenched the flames; while the faithful sepoys gave their assailants a reception which forced them again to flee. But hope came not with the victory. The troops were ill from fatigue, and exposure to the drenching rains and burning suns of August; and worse still, they were utterly disheartened. The provisions, which had not been stored with a view to so great a number, had been dealt out sparingly for the last day, and were now nearly exhausted; and the entire company, men, women and children, drooped in almost hopeless discouragement. It was impossible to convey intelligence to Mergui or Maulmain, for the single brig lying at anchor was not sea-worthy; and though a small junk had been wrested from a company of Chinamen, there was no hope of being able to get it under way with a living man on board. With the light of day, the firing from the wall again commenced, and continued almost incessantly; and now death seemed to be looking into the crowded building from every quarter.

It was after sunrise, when the young physician came hastily, and beckoned Mrs. Burney to the door. A little cloud, like smoke, had appeared in the horizon; and the lady trembled as she had not, at the firing of the cannon or the attacks of the enemy.

"I think—I think—I do not know!" she exclaimed, hurriedly; while eager gazers gathered near, and fixed their eyes on the same object.

"The steamer! the steamer!" at length was the simultaneous cry, and the air resounded with shouts of joy. As Col. Burney leaped to the wharf in the most profound astonishment at the strange uproar, he encountered his wife and infant child, then glanced his eye on the swarming building, then up to the city wall, and he comprehended at once the whole scene. The energetic officer lost not a moment's time; and long before the sun set, the little steam-vessel was puffing on her way back to Maulmain, with the two worn-out ladies resting (oh! what a luxury was that rest!) in her cabin. Several shots were fired after her, as she left the wharf, but the balls either missed their aim, or spent themselves on the water. Great was the consternation when the news reached Maulmain. The roll of the drum was heard all night in the busy cantonments; and by peep of day, the vessel was again under way, laden with European soldiers.

In the meantime, neither Col. Burney nor his men had been idle. His presence infused new life into the troops; and many of the sick crept from their damp, moldy mats, and took their places again in the ranks. He immediately commenced throwing up a breast-work; but the firing from the wall was such a constant source of annoyance, that he at last conceived the bold design of scaling it, and taking possession of the guns. Followed by a trusty band of sepoys, he was under the walls, before the rebels had suspected his intentions; and with a rapidity of movement for which they were entirely unprepared, and which stupified them, by its unexpectedness, he commenced his ascent. Just as his head appeared above the wall a well-aimed blow sent him reeling backward, but he scarce lost his footing, and though stunned and half-blinded, he was almost the first to encounter the few who dared to resist the assault. In a few moments the jinjal, which had occasioned the most trouble, was hurled from its position, and with the other guns was instantly conveyed to the wharf by the now friendly Chinese. Elated by this success, neither the officer nor his men could sit down quietly and wait for assistance; and so, by the time Maulmain was ringing with the news of the revolt, Tavoy was in possession of the brave Englishman and his faithful sepoys. In an incredibly short time, the bold leader of the revolt, (who boasted royal blood, and had built his plans on a broader basis than was at the time suspected) was seized, and with several of his companions, received sentence of death, from a court-martial. And while Mr. Boardman stepped aside to hide his own emotion, as well as to escape the entreaties with which the poor wretches assailed him, as they clung to his knees, in the agony of their despair, four human beings passed from the flush and strength of manhood, into an eternity of which they had scarce heard. The city prison, too, was crowded with rebels, awaiting the sentence of a civil tribunal; and thirty of these afterward shared the fate of their leader and his companions.

All property that could not be appropriated, had been cut to pieces and destroyed, in the most wanton manner; and while those who had fled to the wharf, were endeavoring to find something worth saving in the wreck of their goods, the other inhabitants were coming in, family by family, with the white flag of peace in their hands. And thus the reinforcement from Maulmain found those whom they had expected to deliver from an extremity of peril, gayly wearing the laurels which imagination had already twined around their own brows.

The infant of the English lady was of an age too tender to survive scenes like the foregoing; and soon after gaining a place of safety, it closed its eyes in death. But Mrs. Boardman's little George seemed almost miraculously to have escaped from harm. His illness had made her doubly vigilant, and she had guarded him night and day, with unsurpassed care, placing her own bosom between him and every kind of suffering. It was to this unceasing watchfulness, perhaps, that she owed the long, tedious illness, which ensued, during the four or five months previous to the birth of a second son, the bud already mentioned, as having been so early twined in the same wreath with his sainted sister.[1] And there was yet another sufferer. The suffocating air, the damp, dirty floor, and the walls all dripping with moisture, were laden with consumption to those whose constitutions were predisposed to this most insidious of diseases; and Mr. Boardman's cough grew hollow, his voice husky, the shadow beneath his eye darker, the cheek more glowing, the eye more brilliant, the frame weaker, and heavy with faintness, and the spirit purer and more enthusiastic. He was very near his eternal home.

1 This child, which died at the age of nine and a half months, was named Judson Wade; and thus, rather oddly, bore, in the order of their seniority in the mission, the names of the three who had been associated at Amherst and Maulmain.

Chapter 9

WITHERING AND WATCHING

"Come to the land of peace!
Come where the tempest hath no longer sway,
The shadow passes from the soul away,
The sounds of weeping cease!"
—*Mrs. Hemans.*

The angel-call, to which the sweet poetess has given words, was written on lip, cheek, and forehead of the failing missionary; but yet the fire of life went out so slowly, spark by spark, that the process was for a long time scarce visible to any, but the eye of love. He still pursued his labors with ever-growing enthusiasm—now itinerating about the villages bordering Tavoy, and now taking a long tour among the Karen mountains, until compelled to forego these spirit-stirring employments and watch by the pillow of his suffering wife. In January, Mrs. Boardman appeared to be upon the verge of the grave. A little after she rallied slightly; and in March took a trip to Maulmain, where she still continued to improve. In April she was joined by her husband; his presence being necessary to supply, in some degree, the places of Messrs. Judson and Wade, who had left their station, for a time, in favor of Burmah Proper.

In June, Mrs. Boardman thus writes a friend, "My dear husband is suffering from a distressing cough, which the doctor says is undoubtedly occasioned by an affection of the lungs. It was brought on by our dreadful exposures and sufferings during the rebellion; and, I think, much increased by the hardships he endured in his village-preaching at Tavoy. He used sometimes to walk twenty miles in a day, preaching and teaching as he went, and at night have no shelter but an open zayat, no food at all calculated to sustain his failing nature, and no bed, but a straw mat spread on the cold, open bamboo floor."

And now came the indescribably mournful watch, when the aching heart feels its one earthly support crumbling, sand by sand, from beneath it, and there is none to raise a saving finger. But still the toil went on even now—Mr. Boardman preaching, attending Scriptural recitations, and prayer-meetings, overseeing the printing of books, preparing lessons for the boys' school, etc. etc., and Mrs. Boardman, assisted by Mrs. Bennett, who had lately arrived, busy in her own scarcely less important province. In November they returned to Tavoy, and from the cabin of the vessel, which conveyed them thither, thus speaks the sorrowful watcher:—"Oh, my dear mother, it would distress you to see how emaciated he is!—and so weak, that he is scarce able to move. . . . God is calling to me in a most impressive manner, to set my heart on heavenly things. Two lovely infants already in the world of bliss—my beloved husband suffering under a disease, which will most assuredly take him from me—my own health poor, and little Georgie often ill. Oh, how little have I to attach me to this wretched, fallen world!"

They were welcomed to Tavoy by affectionate hearts—especially the simple, grateful Karens, who flocked to them in crowds from their homes in the wilderness. Mrs. Boardman thus makes mention of this singular people, in a letter, bearing date January 10th, 1831:

"They" (the Karens) "had heard of Mr. Boardman's illness; and the sadness depicted on their countenances, when they saw him so pale and emaciated, affected me much. I felt that God had, indeed, raised me up sympathizing friends, even in the wilderness, among those who are considered barbarians by the Burmans themselves. Before we had been here a fortnight, one party came for the sole purpose of seeing us and hearing the gospel. They remained four days, and the eagerness with which they listened to our instructions, and the deep interest they manifested in religious affairs, reminded us of our associations at home.

The three first days were spent in examining candidates for baptism, and conversing with, and instructing those who had previously been baptized. Sometimes Mr. Boardman sat up in a chair, and addressed them for a few moments; but oftener, I sat on his sick couch, and interpreted his feeble whispers. He was nearly overcome by the gladdening prospect, and frequently wept. But the most touchingly interesting time was the day before they left us, when nineteen were baptized. . . . Our road lay through that part of the town which is filled with monasteries; and over the huge brick walls we could see multitudes of priests and noviciates looking at us—I doubt not with mingled scorn and hatred. As to the common people they reviled us openly, and in so cruel a manner, that my heart was ready to burst. Mr. Boardman was too ill to walk or ride on horseback, and there being no other mode of conveyance in the town, the Karens carried him out on his little cot. 'See!' said the revilers, in bitter ridicule, to two Tavoyan disciples, 'see your teacher!—a living man carried as if he were already dead!' But I will not shock your feelings by repeating their taunts. We pitied them, and passed on in silence. At length we reached a beautiful pond, nearly a mile in circumference, and bordered by green trees. Here we stopped—a party of about fifty in number—and kneeling on the grass, implored the Divine blessing. Then Moung Ing[1] administered the ordinance of baptism to nineteen believers, who were, a little time ago, in utter ignorance of the true God. . . . During this scene, grief and joy alternately took possession of my breast. To see so many in this dark, heathen land 'putting on Christ,' could but fill me with joy and gratitude; but when I looked at my beloved husband, lying

1 One of the earliest Rangoon disciples, and the second native that was ordained. He had been sent to Mergui, by the Maulmain Missionaries, and, fortunately, touched at Tavoy in time to render Mr. B. an important service.

pale on his couch, and recollected the last time we stood by those waters, my heart could not but be sad at the contrast. It was on a similar occasion, and the surrounding mountains echoed with his voice, as he pronounced the words, 'I baptize thee,' etc. Now his strength was exhausted, his voice was weak; and the thought that I should no more see him administer this blessed ordinance, filled me with inexpressible grief. But in the evening, when we came together to receive from him the emblems of our Saviour's sufferings, my feelings changed. He made an effort; and God helped him to go through with the exercises alone, and without any apparent injury to his health. A breathless silence pervaded the room, excepting the sound of his voice, which was so low and feeble, that it seemed to carry the assurance that we should feast no more together, till we met in our Father's kingdom. When he handed us the cup, it was to me, as though our Saviour had been in the midst, and I could say,

'How sweet and awful is the place,
With Christ within the doors!'

The grief and anguish, which I felt at the baptism, had subsided into a calm; and in contemplating the agonies of our blessed Redeemer, I, for a moment, forgot the bitter cup preparing for myself."

Oh! what a blessed resource has the Christian! what a sure anchor! Though every earthly stay be wrested from the fainting heart, if it but turn from the "broken reed" to Heaven, it will find a pillar of strength, which cannot fail. Against this stand the mightiest soldiers of the Cross, the Pauls and the Luthers in the Christian field; the poor, unknown widow leans on this, when her children cry to her for bread, which she cannot give, and yet her heart keeps back from breaking; and to this clung the lone missionary's wife, when she listened to the faltering accents of that voice, which she had loved in its strength, and forgot, even as she listened, the "bitter cup" preparing for her. This, too, was the support of the dying sufferer, while his spirit increased each day in loveliness, as though it had already caught some of the hues of the beautiful land which it was silently approaching. "He exhibited," says the watching wife, "a tenderness of spirit, a holy sensibility, such as I never witnessed before. He seemed to see the goodness of God in everything. He would weep while conversing on the love of Jesus; and words cannot describe to you the depth of feeling with which he spoke of his own unworthiness."

The year closed, and another one opened, and yet the missionary lingered; for a few more sheaves were to be given him on earth, before he received his crown in the Paradise of ransomed spirits. How different from the commencement of the preceding year! Then Mrs. Boardman was the sufferer, and her husband wrote—"She still grows weaker, and her case is now more alarming. All missionary labor has been suspended for a week, to allow me all my time in taking care of her. I have written to Maulmain for some of our friends to come to our assistance, and be with us, at this critical time; and we hope they will be able and disposed to comply with the request. Should they come even immediately, I can scarcely hope for their arrival before the crisis, or probably, fatal termination, of my dear partner's disorder. My comfort, in my present affliction is the thought, that if to our former trials, the Lord sees fit to add that of removing my beloved companion, He does it with a perfect knowledge of all the blessedness, which death, in its consequences, will confer on *her,* and of all the sorrows and distresses which her loss will occasion her bereaved husband and orphan children, in the peculiarities of our present condition. It affords me great relief to have been assured by her, that the bitterness of death is past, and that heavenly glories have been unfolded in a wonderful and unexpected manner to her view."

And now Mrs. Boardman had the same sorrow and the same consolations. Her strength had increased, as her toils grew more numerous, and the burden on her spirit heavier; and she had the satisfaction of finding herself equal to the performance of her sweetly painful duties. Among the last traces of her dying husband's pen, are these words, addressed to a sister:

"During my present protracted illness, and especially when I was at the worst stage, she was the tenderest, most assiduous, attentive and affectionate of nurses. Without her, I think I should have finished my career in a few days. And even when our lamented, darling babe lay struggling in the very arms of death, though she was with him constantly, night and day, she did not allow me to suffer one moment, for lack of her attentions. I cannot write what I feel on this tender subject. But oh! what kindness in our Heavenly Father, that when her services were so much needed, her health was preserved, and she had strength given her to perform her arduous labors."

Chapter 10

"DEATH IN THE JUNGLE"

"Oh! is it not a noble thing to die,
As dies the Christian, with his armor on!—"
—*Willis.*

In January, 1831, the Rev. Francis Mason arrived at Tavoy. On the jetty, reclining helplessly in the chair which had served the purpose of a carriage, a pale, worn-out man, with "the characters of death in his countenance," waited to welcome his successor.

"You have come in time, my brother," was the language of his glance, as he extended his emaciated, colorless hand; and so, indeed, he had.

In eight days after, the little family was on its way to the Karen wilderness, and Mr. Mason made one of the party. When they returned, a corpse was borne upon a litter, which had conveyed the invalid from the town. We leave the tale to another pen.

LETTER FROM MRS. BOARDMAN.

Tavoy, March 7, 1831.

"My beloved Parents:

"With a heart glowing with joy, and at the same time rent with anguish unutterable, I take my pen to address you. You, too, will rejoice when you hear what God has wrought through the instrumentality of your beloved son. Yes, you will bless God that you were enabled to devote him to this blessed service among the heathen, when I tell you that within the last two months, fifty-seven have been baptized, all Karens, excepting one, a little boy of the school and son of the native governor. Twenty-three were baptized in this city by Moung Ing, and thirty-four in their native wilderness by Mr. Mason.

"Mr. Mason arrived Jan. 23rd, and on the 31st, he, with Mr. Boardman, myself and George, set out on a long-promised tour among the Karens. Mr. Boardman was very feeble, but we hoped the change of air and scenery would be beneficial. A company of Karens had come to convey us out, Mr. Boardman on his bed, and me in a chair. We reached the place on the third day, and found they had erected a bamboo chapel on a beautiful stream at the base of a range of mountains. The place was central, and nearly one hundred persons had assembled, more than half of them applicants for baptism. Oh it was a sight calculated to call forth the liveliest joy of which human nature is susceptible, and made me, for a moment, forget my bitter griefs—a sight far surpassing all I had ever anticipated, even in my most sanguine hours. The Karens cooked, ate and slept on the ground, by the riverside, with no other shelter than the trees of the forest. Three years ago they were sunk in the lowest depths of ignorance and superstition. Now the glad tidings of mercy had reached them, and they were willing to live in the open air, away from their homes, for the sake of enjoying the privileges of the Gospel.

"My dear husband had borne the journey better than we had feared, though he suffered from exhaustion and pain in his side, which, however, was much relieved by a little attention. His spirits were unusually good, and we fondly hoped that a few days' residence in that delightful, airy spot, surrounded by his loved Karens, would recruit and invigorate his weakened frame. But I soon perceived he was failing, and tenderly urged his return to town, where he could enjoy the quiet of home, and the benefit of medical advice. But he repelled the thought at once, saying he confidently expected improvement from the change, and that the disappointment would be worse for him than staying. 'And even,' added he, 'should my poor, unprofitable life be somewhat shortened by staying, ought I, on that account merely, to leave this interesting field? Should I not rather stay and assist in gathering in these dear scattered lambs of the fold? You know, Sarah, that coming on a foreign mission involves the probability of a shorter life, than staying in one's native country. And yet obedience to our Lord, and compassion for the perishing heathen, induced us to make this sacrifice. And have we ever repented that we came? No; I trust we can both say bless God for bringing us to Burmah, for directing our footsteps to Tavoy, and even for leading us hither. You already know, my love,' he continued, with a look of tenderness never to be forgotten, 'that I cannot live long, I must sink under this disease; and should we go home now, the all-important business which brought us out, must be given up, and I might linger out a few days of suffering, stung with the reflection, that I had preferred a few idle days, to my Master's service. Do not, therefore, ask me to go, till these poor Karens have been baptized.' I saw he was right, but my feelings revolted. Nothing seemed so valuable as his life, and I felt that I could make any sacrifice to prolong it, though it were but for one hour. Still a desire to gratify him, if no higher motive, made me silent, though my heart ached to see him so ill in such a wretched place, deprived of many of the comforts of life, to say nothing of the indulgencies desirable in sickness.

"The chapel was large, but open on all sides, excepting a small place built up for Mr. Mason, and a room about five feet wide and ten feet long, for the accommodation of Mr. Boardman and myself with our little boy. The roof was so low, that I could not stand upright; and it was but poorly enclosed, so that he was exposed to the burning rays of the sun by day, and to the cold winds and damp fog by night. But his mind was happy, and he would often say, 'If I live to see this one ingathering, I may well exclaim, with happy Simeon, Lord, now lettest thou thy servant depart in peace, according to thy word, for mine eyes have seen thy salvation. How many ministers have wished they might die in their pulpits; and would not, dying in a spot like this, be even more blessed than dying in a pulpit at home? I feel that it would.'

"Nor was it merely the pleasing state of things around him that filled his mind with comfort. He would sometimes dwell on the infinite compassion of God, and his own unworthiness, till his strength was quite exhausted; and though he told Mr. Mason that he had not the rapture which he had sometimes enjoyed, yet his mind was calm and peaceful; and it was plainly perceptible, that earthly passions had died away, and that he was enjoying sweet foretastes of that rest into which he was so soon to enter. He would often say to me, 'My meditations are very sweet, though my mind seems as much weakened as my body. I have not had that liveliness of feeling, which I have sometimes enjoyed, owing to my great weakness, but I shall soon be released from shackles, and be where I can praise God continually, without weariness. My thoughts delight to dwell on these words, *There is no night there.*'

"I felt that the time of separation was fast approaching, and said to him, 'My dear, I have one request to make; it is, that you would pray much for George, during your few remaining days. I shall soon be left alone, almost the only one on earth to pray for him, and I have great confidence in your dying prayers.' He looked earnestly at the little boy, and said, 'I will try to pray for him; but I trust very many prayers will ascend for the dear child from our friends at home, who will be induced to supplicate the more earnestly for him, when they hear that he is left fatherless in a heathen land.'

"On Wednesday, while looking in the glass, he seemed at once to see symptoms of his approaching dissolution, and said, without emotion, 'I have altered greatly—I am sinking into the grave very fast—just on the verge.' Mr. Mason said to him, 'Is there nothing we can do for you? Had we not better call the physician? Or shall we try to remove you into town immediately?' After a few moments' deliberation, it was concluded to defer the baptism of the male applicants, and set out for home early the next morning. Nearly all the female candidates had been examined, and as it is difficult for them to come to town, it was thought best that Mr. Mason should baptize them in the evening. We knelt, and Mr. Mason having prayed for a blessing on the decision, we sat down to breakfast with sorrowful hearts.

"While we were at the table, my beloved husband said, 'I shall soon be thrown away for this world; but I hope the Lord Jesus will take me up. That merciful Being, who is represented as passing by, and having compassion on the poor cast-out infant, will not suffer me to perish. O, I have no hope but in the wonderful, condescending, infinite mercy of God, through his dear Son. I cast my poor perishing soul, loaded with sin, as it is, upon his compassionate arms, assured that all will be forever safe.' On seeing my tears, he said, 'Are you not reconciled to the will of God, my love?' When I told him I hoped I did not feel unreconciled, he continued, 'I have long ago, and many times, committed you and our little one into the hands of our covenant God. He is the husband of the widow and the father of the fatherless. *Leave thy fatherless children, I will preserve them alive; and let thy widows trust in me,* saith the Lord. He will be your stay and support, when I am gone. The separation will be but short. O, how happy I shall be to welcome you to heaven.' He then addressed Mr. Mason, as follows:—'Brother, I am heartily rejoiced, and bless God that you have arrived, and especially am I gratified, that you are so much interested for the poor Karens. You will, I am assured, watch over them, and take care of them; and if some of them turn back, you will still care for them. As to my dear wife and child, I know you will do all in your power to make them comfortable. Mrs. B. will probably spend the ensuing rains in Tavoy. She will be happy with you and Mrs. Mason; that is, as happy as she can be in her state of loneliness. She will mourn for me, and a widow's state is desolate and sorrowful at best. But God will be infinitely better to her, than I have ever been.' On the same day, he wished me to read some hymns on affliction, sickness, death, etc. I took Wesley's Hymn Book, the only one we had with us, and read several, among others, the one beginning, 'Ah, lovely appearance of death.'

"On Wednesday evening, thirty-four persons were baptized. Mr. Boardman was carried to the water side, though so weak that he could hardly breathe without the continual use of the fan and the smelling-bottle. The joyful sight was almost too much for his feeble frame. When we reached the chapel, he said he would like to sit up and take tea with us. We placed his cot near the table, and having bolstered him up, we took tea together. He asked the blessing, and did it with his right hand upraised, and in a tone that struck me to the heart. It was the same tremulous, yet urgent, and I had almost said, unearthly voice, with which my aged grandfather used to pray. We now began to notice that brightening of the mental faculties, which I had heard spoken of, in persons near their end.

"After tea was removed, all the disciples present, about fifty in number, gathered around him, and he addressed them for a few moments in language like the following:—'I did hope to stay with you till after Lord's-day, and administer to you once more the Lord's Supper. But God is calling me away from you. I am about to die, and shall soon be inconceivably happy in heaven. When I am gone, remember what I have taught you; and O, be careful to persevere unto the end, that when you die, we may meet one another in the presence of God, never more to part. Listen to the word of the new teacher and the teacheress as you have done to mine. The teacheress will be very much distressed. Strive to lighten her burdens, and comfort her by your good conduct. Do not neglect prayer. The eternal God, to whom you pray, is unchangeable. Earthly teachers sicken and die, but God remains forever the same. Love Jesus Christ with all your hearts, and you will be forever safe.' This address I gathered from the Karens, as I was absent preparing his things for the night. Having rested a few minutes, he offered a short prayer, and then with Mr. Mason's assistance, distributed tracts and portions of Scripture to them all. Early the next morning we left for home, accompanied by nearly all the males and some of the females, the remainder returning to their homes in the wilderness. Mr. Boardman was free from pain during the day, and there was no unfavorable change, except that his mouth grew sore. But at four o'clock in the afternoon, we were overtaken by a violent shower of rain, accompanied by lightning and thunder. There was no house in sight, and we were obliged to remain in the open air, exposed to the merciless storm. We covered him with mats and blankets, and held our umbrellas over him, all to no purpose. I was obliged to stand and see the storm beating upon him, till his mattress and pillows were drenched with rain. We hastened on, and soon came to a Tavoy house. The inhabitants at first refused us admittance, and we ran for shelter into the out-houses. The shed I happened to enter, proved to be the house of their gods, and thus I committed an almost unpardonable offence. After some persuasion they admitted us into the house, or rather verandah, for they would not allow us to sleep inside, though I begged the privilege for my sick husband with tears. In ordinary cases, perhaps, they would have been hospitable; but they knew that Mr. Boardman was a teacher of a foreign religion, and that the Karens in our company had embraced that religion.

"At evening worship, Mr. Boardman requested Mr. Mason to read the thirty-fourth Psalm. He seemed almost spent, and said, 'This poor perishing dust will soon be laid in the grave; but God can employ other lumps of clay to perform his will, as easily as he has this poor unworthy one.' I told him, I should like to sit up and watch by him, but he objected, and said in a tender supplicating tone, 'cannot we sleep together?' The rain still continued, and his cot was wet, so that he was obliged to lie on the bamboo floor. Having found a place where our little boy could sleep without danger of falling through openings in the floor, I threw myself down, without undressing, beside my beloved husband. I spoke to him often during the night, and he said he felt well, excepting an uncomfortable feeling in his mouth and throat. This was somewhat relieved by frequent washings with cold water. Miserably wretched as his situation was, he did not complain; on the contrary, his heart seemed overflowing with gratitude. 'O,' said he, 'how kind and good our Father in heaven is to me; how many are racked with pain, while I, though near the grave, am almost free from distress of body. I suffer nothing, *nothing* to what you, my dear Sarah, had to endure last year, when I thought I must lose you. And then I have you to move me so tenderly. I should have sunk into the grave ere this, but for your assiduous attention. And brother Mason is as kind to me as if he were my own brother. And then how many, in addition to pain of body, have anguish of soul, while my mind is sweetly stayed on God.' On my saying, 'I hope we shall be at home tomorrow night, where you can lie on your comfortable bed, and I can nurse you as I wish,' he said, 'I want nothing that the world can afford, but my wife and friends; earthly conveniences and comforts are of little consequence to one so near heaven. I only want them for your sake.' In the morning we thought him a little better, though I perceived, when I gave him his sago, that his breath was very short. He, however, took rather more nourishment than usual, and spoke about the manner of his conveyance home. We ascertained that by waiting until twelve o'clock, we could go the greater part of the way by water.

"At about nine o'clock, his hands and feet grew cold, and the affectionate Karens rubbed them all the forenoon, excepting a few moments when he requested to be left alone. At ten o'clock, he was much distressed for breath, and I thought the long dreaded moment had arrived. I asked him, if he felt as if he was going home—'not just yet,' he replied. On giving him a little wine and water, he revived. Shortly after, he said, 'you were alarmed without cause, just now, dear—I know the reason of the distress I felt, but am too weak to explain it to you.' In a few moments he said to me, 'Since you spoke to me about George, I have prayed for him almost incessantly—more than in all my life before.'

"It drew near twelve, the time for us to go to the boat. We were distressed at the thought of removing him, when evidently so near the last struggle, though we did not think it so near as it really was. But there was no alternative. The chilling frown of the iron-faced Tavoyan was to us as if he was continually saying, 'be gone.' I wanted a little broth for my expiring husband, but on asking them for a fowl they said they had none, though at that instant, on glancing my eye through an opening in the floor, I saw three or four under the house. My heart was well nigh breaking.

"We hastened to the boat, which was only a few steps from the house. The Karens carried Mr. Boardman first, and as the shore was muddy, I was obliged to wait till they could return for me. They took me immediately to him; but O, the agony of my soul, when I saw the hand of death was on him! He was looking me full in the face, but his eyes were changed, not dimmed, but brightened, and the pupils so dilated, that I feared he could not see me. I spoke to him—kissed him—but he made no return, though I fancied that he tried to move his lips. I pressed his hand, knowing that if he could, he would return the pressure; but, alas! for the first time, he was insensible to my love, and forever. I had brought a glass of wine and water already mixed, and a smelling-bottle, but neither was of any avail to him now. Agreeably to a previous request, I called the faithful Karens, who loved him so much, and whom he had loved unto death, to come and watch his last gentle breathings, for there was no struggle.

"Never, my dear parents, did one of our poor fallen race have less to contend with, in the last enemy. Little George was brought to see his dying father, but he was too young to know there was cause for grief. When Sarah died, her father said to George, 'Poor little boy, you will not know tomorrow what you have lost today.' A deep pang rent my bosom at the recollection of this, and a still deeper one succeeded when the thought struck me, that though my little boy may not know tomorrow what he has lost today, yet when years have rolled by, and he shall have felt the unkindness of a deceitful, selfish world, *he will know*.

"Mr. Mason wept, and the sorrowing Karens knelt down in prayer to God—that God, of whom their expiring teacher had taught them—that God, into whose presence the emancipated spirit was just entering—that God with whom they hope and expect to be happy forever. My own feelings I will not attempt to describe. You may have some faint idea of them, when you recollect what he was to me, how tenderly I loved him, and, at the same time, bear in mind the precious promises to the afflicted.

"We came in silence down the river, and landed about three miles from our house. The Karens placed his precious remains on his little bed, and with feelings which you can better imagine than I describe, we proceeded homewards. The mournful intelligence had reached town before us, and we were soon met by Moung Ing, the Burman preacher. At the sight of us, he burst into a flood of tears. Next, we met the two native Christian sisters, who lived with us. But the moment of most bitter anguish was yet to come on our arrival at the house. They took him into the sleeping room, and when I uncovered his face, for a few moments, nothing was heard but reiterated sobs. He had not altered—the same sweet smile, with which he was wont to welcome me, sat on his countenance. His eyes had opened in bringing him, and all present seemed expecting to hear his voice; when the thought, that it was silent forever, rushed upon us, and filled us with anguish sudden and unutterable. There were the Burman Christians, who had listened so long, with edification and delight, to his preaching—there were the Karens, who looked to him as their guide, their earthly all—there were the scholars whom he had taught the way to heaven, and the Christian sisters, whose privilege it had been to wash, as it were, his feet.

Early next morning, his funeral was attended, and all the Europeans in the place, with many natives, were present. It may be some consolation to you to know that everything was performed in as decent a manner, as if he had been buried in our own dear native land. By his own request, he was interred on the south side of our darling first-born. It is a pleasant circumstance to me, that they sleep *side by side*. But it is infinitely more consoling to think, that their glorified spirits have met in that blissful world, where sin and death never enter, and sorrow is unknown.

"Praying that we may be abundantly prepared to enter into our glorious rest, I remain, my dear parents, your deeply afflicted, but most affectionate child,

"SARAH H. BOARDMAN."

And so the sorrowing, rejoicing mourner way left alone. Alone? No, there was the smiling, fatherless boy, who could not know his loss; there were the kind, affectionate strangers, whose pitying lips dropped with consolation, but whose hearts, like her own a few years previous, were yet unchastened by affliction; there were the weeping Christians, like untaught children, clamorous in their grief; but, above all, there was He, the Holy One, who, in wisdom and in love, had dealt the terrible blow. Oh, no! the bereaved mourner was not alone; for God was there, and her hushed, subdued heart felt his presence.

"Death now seems nearer to me, and Heaven dearer," she says, in a letter to a friend, "than before I was afflicted; and I do feel that my heart is more set on things above than it formerly was. Oh! I see and feel that my afflictions are of precisely the kind my soul needed. 'Though He slay me, yet will I trust in Him.' . . . I receive from my dear friends, the Masons, every possible kindness. But alas! the hours of loneliness and bitter weeping that I endure, are known only to God. But still Jesus has sweetened the cup, and I would not that it should have passed my lip."

Again she says, administering consolation in her own generous, thoughtful way, to those who she knew would grieve for her on the other side of the world: "It is true I have lost my guide, my earthly all; but, my dear parents, is not God infinitely better to us than the nearest and dearest of earthly friends? I can appeal to you both with confidence, for you know how sweet it is to draw nigh to God. I trust you have both, many times been so near heaven, while engaged in prayer, that you have forgotten all your earthly sorrows. And this, my beloved parents, is sometimes the case with me even now, when I am suffering under the greatest possible affliction that my Heavenly Father could have allotted me. The sweet promises of God are precious to my soul; and I look forward with joy to the blissful moment, when I shall go to be for ever united with my dear husband and children, in a world where there is no sorrow nor weeping."

The following poem was written some time after, at Yalah, a romantic place on the seashore, which she had often visited with her husband. It was her favorite scene; and its principal features, to which she alludes in the verses, have been more distinctly defined in a pencil sketch, taken during one of these visits.

"The moon throws her bright and glistening ray
On ocean's heaving breast;
And with her light is the landscape gay,—
But to me, 'tis in sable dressed.

For the eye is dim, and the voice is hushed,
That with me admired the scene;
And present enjoyments all are crushed,
'Neath the tread of those that have been.

The ocean rolls on in sullen pride,
As for ages past he has done;
But my guide over life's more fearful tide,
The friend of my youth, is gone.

The tree, to which the frail creeper clung,
Still lifts its stately head;
But he, on whom my spirit hung,
Is sleeping with the dead.

The evening star sheds her silvery light,
Bright orbs in their beauty roll;
But to me 'tis a dark and dreary night,
For quenched is the star of my soul.

'Tis long since they bore thee away from me,
And laid thee low in the grave;
But could I forget thee, my soul would be,
Like the rock that repels the wave.

And oh, thou departed and sainted one,
In thy robes of glory clad;
Dost thou e'er, from thy bright abode, look down,
On me deserted and sad?

Oh, thine is indeed a bright abode!
And brilliant thy diadem—
The crown of life from the hand of God,
Adorned with many a gem.

For thou didst bear the gospel light
To the heathen world afar;
And the darkness of their moral night
Gave way to the Morning Star.

The youths of China learned of thee
To seek a Saviour's face;
And the ruder Burman at thy knee
Heard the tale of sovereign grace.

And who are the crowds with visage meek,
That come from the mountains high,
The tear of penitence warm on each cheek,
And hope in every eye?

There is manhood, and age with hoary head,
And the child, scarce touched with guile,
And the forest-maid, from whose native shade,
Nor love nor pleasure could wile.

The Karens, for whom thy parting breath
Went forth in fervent prayer,
Who knelt beside thy bed of death,
Are thy crown of gladness there.

A sound, as from some, heavenly shrine,
Comes sweetly floating near,
And accents mild and soft like thine,
Fall gently on my ear.

Chapter 11

THE FEMALE MISSIONARY

"Toiling—rejoicing—sorrowing,"
The Christian "onward goes;
Each morning sees some task begin,
Each evening sees it close;
Something attempted, something done,
Has earned a night's repose."
—*Longfellow.*

I have been trying," said the lone widow, in a note to a missionary friend, "with fasting, and prayers, and tears, to inquire what my duty is, about going home soon with little George. I feel conscious of the weakness of my own judgment; and am about writing to Maulmain, Rangoon, and Mergui, to ask the advice of my brethren and sisters." But before these letters had been despatched, she received the following, from a missionary, then in Rangoon—one who knew from his own bitter experience, all the depths of her sufferings, and all the points which the finger of sympathy might dare to touch. After saying, "I can only advise you to take the cup with both hands, and sit down quietly to the bitter repast, which God has appointed for your sanctification;"—"You will soon learn there is sweetness at the bottom;"—"You will find heaven coming near to you; and familiarity with your husband's voice will be a connecting link, drawing you almost within the sphere of celestial music," etc., etc. The writer adds, "As to little Georgie, who has now no earthly father to care for him—you cannot, of course, part with him at present. But if you should wish to send him home, I pledge myself to use what little influence I have, in procuring for him all those advantages of education, which your fondest wishes can desire. Or, if you should be prematurely taken away, and should condescend on your dying bed, to commit him to me, by the briefest line or verbal message, I hereby pledge my fidelity, to receive and treat him as my own son, to send him home in the best time and way, to provide for his education, and to watch over him as long as I live." Then follow suggestions for her own personal comfort; and all this, coming as it did long before American friends could learn anything of her afflictions, was a source of inexpressible relief. And so, by the time the invitation to return the happy home of her childhood reached her, she was prepared to give a decisive answer.

"When I first stood by the grave of my husband, I thought that I must go home with George. But these poor, inquiring, and Christian Karens, and the school-boys, and the Burmese Christians, would then be left without any one to instruct them; and the poor, stupid Tavoyans would go on in the road to death, with no one to warn them of their danger. How then, oh, how can I go? We shall not be separated long. A few more years, and we shall all meet in yonder blissful world, whither those we love have gone before us." "I feel thankful that I was allowed to come to this heathen land. Oh, it is a precious privilege to tell idolaters of the Gospel; and when we see them disposed to love the Saviour, we forget all our privations and dangers. My beloved husband wore out his life in this glorious cause; and that remembrance makes me more than ever attached to the work, and the people for whose salvation he labored till death."

And in the midst of her sorrow, suffering, and loneliness, the fond mother's heart could devise no higher wish for the child of her love, her "only one," as she often touchingly names little George, than that "the 'dew of his youth' might be consecrated to the living God, and that, at some future day, he might stand in his father's place, and preach among the heathen the unsearchable riches of Christ." That he might devote his young life to those who jeered the parent, when disease had shorn him of his strength, and refused the shelter of a roof to his dying head! Surely, the noblest Roman matron could never have aspired to heroism like this. *She* taught her son to die stoically, with the stain of his enemy's blood upon his sword, and went through life without conceiving the possibility of a higher flight.

For three years previous to the death of her husband, Mrs. Boardman had been almost constantly ill; and this, together with the illness of her family, by which her cares were greatly increased, prevented her engaging but slightly in direct missionary labor. Beside, the station had been twice broken up, and all operations suspended; and this was ruinous to the prospects of the few schools she had succeeded in establishing. Sometimes she conversed a little with visitors; but her husband was better qualified for the task; and he was free from the small necessary cares, which, in Burmah, triple the weight of a woman's usual domestic duties. She had made an effort to establish day-schools; and these had, at times, been prosperous, though at other times they were entirely broken up. She had also kept the boys' boarding-school in existence—bare existence; for, at the time of her husband's death, it was very small indeed. But when she was left alone, with the wild, simple mountaineers flocking about her, and looking to her lips for the words which were to renovate their natures; when she turned to the Tavoyans, and considered that even among them, impudent and reckless as they were in their ignorance, might lie, unrecognized, some beautiful stone, to be cut and polished for the temple of the Eternal—when she looked about her, and thought of all these things, she began, more than ever, to feel and

"Know how sublime a thing it is,
To suffer and be strong."

Mrs. Chaplin, in one of her beautiful letters, after speaking of the "triumphal ascension" of the sainted husband, adds, "I rejoice that as he went up, his mantle descended upon you, his beloved one—and that your missionary zeal was kindled at this altar, and that more than ever before, it is in your heart to benefit the heathen." In truth, such a mantle, so heavy with important duties, seldom weighs upon the shoulders of a woman; and very seldom is it worn with such a modest, unconscious grace. So light was her step, that even those who looked upon her daily, scarce suspected she was treading in the foot-prints of the Christian warrior; the sword of truth was so concealed by the flowers of gentleness, and by gospel balms, that when it made its presence felt none knew the hand that wielded it; and so unassuming were her feminine adornments, and worn with such sweet simplicity, that the "armor of proof" beneath, was completely hidden in their graceful folds. But the light foot was firm and daring; the armor was never thrown aside; and the small spirit-sword had a keen, resistless point.

To a friend she says, "Every moment of my time is occupied, from sunrise till ten o'clock in the evening. And now, although I would fain write you a long letter, I scarce know how to find time for a single line. It is late bed-time, and I am surrounded by five Karen women, three of whom arrived this afternoon from the jungle, after having been separated from us nearly five months by the heavy rains. The Karens are beginning to come to us in companies; and with them, and our scholars in the town, and the care of my darling boy, you will scarce think that I have much leisure for letter-writing."

In the same letter, she announces the death of several Christians, one of them a schoolmaster among the Karen mountains. An extract would be wholly irrelevant, but, as exhibiting the nature of the cords which bound her so strongly to this land of darkness, and the near connexion which her employment had with Heaven, it will be pardoned. "Thah-oung," she says, "continued in his school till two days before his death, although he had been for a long time very ill. He felt, then, that he *must* die, and said to his scholars, 'I can do no more—God is calling me away from you—I go into His presence—be not dismayed.' He was then carried to the house of his father, a few miles distant, and there he continued exhorting and praying, to the very last moment. His widow, who is not yet fifteen, is one of the loveliest of our 'desert blossoms.' She and her younger sister, who is also a disciple, have attended Ko Thah-Byoo's school since the death of Thah-oung."

A few extracts from a couple of journal-like letters, published in the Missionary Magazine, for 1832, will give a still better idea of her employments and interests.

"*March*, 1831—One of our best Karen brethren came to see us, and through him, we heard that all the disciples were well; that they were living in love with one another, in the enjoyment of religion, and had nothing to distress them but the death of their beloved teacher. Poor Moung-Quay was obliged to turn away his face to weep several times, while answering my inquiries. Oh, how they feel the stroke that has fallen upon them! And well they may, for he was to them a father and a guide.

"After Mr. Mason left, Mah Doke (the only one of the female converts from Rangoon in these provinces) came in to pray with me. The tears rolled down Mah Men's cheeks as she said, 'I have been telling Moung Shway-bwen, that now you would be more distressed than ever, and he sent me to speak soothing words.' We all knelt down, and it was one of the pleasantest prayer-meetings I ever had."

"A congregation today of nearly thirty listeners. This morning, I was pleased with the simplicity of one of the Karen women. She asked me if I had prayed, not in a way to imply a doubt of my habitual practice of this duty, but in the same simple manner that she would ask if I had eaten breakfast. After the morning service, the female Christians met in my room for prayer, and all took a part—some in Burman, and some in Karen. We were much disturbed by the native music and dancing at a feast, in sight of the house.

Though it was a very splendid entertainment, under an awning, out of doors, not one of our scholars or people showed the least disposition to go, excepting a little Tavoy girl, who had been with me only three days.

"While Moung Ing was preaching, Sek-kike, one of the little Chinese disciples, returned from a visit of two or three weeks, at his grandmother's. He took his seat with the hearers, and the dear child could not help laughing with real delight, at finding himself once more in the midst of the disciples, and under the sound of the gospel. And I confess, when I saw the joy beaming from his countenance, I had as little command over my feelings.

"*December* 31.—The Church at present numbers one hundred and ten members. They are mostly Karens, living at a great distance; and, by their frequent visits to us, over almost impassable mountains and through deserts, the haunt of the tiger, they evince a love for the gospel seldom surpassed. What would the Christians in New-England think of travelling forty or fifty miles on foot, to hear a sermon, and beg a Christian book? A Karen woman, who had been living with us several months, told me, that when she came, the water was so deep she was obliged to wait until the men could fell trees to cross on; and sometimes she forded the streams herself, when the water reached her chin. She said she feared alligators, more than anything else."

From some of the extracts just made, showing the sympathetic disposition of the native Christians, and Mrs. Boardman's affection for them, the truth of some remarks on the heathen character, a few chapters back, may be called in question. But perhaps it will require no more than a sentence from her to show, that it was only as Christians that they were companionable and worthy of affection. "Surely," she says in a note to Mrs. Mason, "it requires the patience of a Job, and the wisdom of a Solomon, to get on with this people, much as I love them, and good as I think they are." Grace does not give those, who have been all their lives shackled in heart and soul, groping in darkness more than Egyptian, at once, the stature of a perfect man; and there can be no more cruel injustice, than stretching the infant disciple on such a Procrustean bed.

In the journal from which the above extracts are made, Mrs. Boardman thus mentions the burning of a Boodhist priest. "The whole town, male and female, from the infant to the gray-headed, are engaged in the ceremonies attendant upon the burning of a priest, who died several months ago. Seven large coffins, perhaps four feet in height, were drawn, on as many cars, adorned with paintings of men and monsters, as large as life, gilded images, looking-glasses, fancy-paper, and a variety of other showy trappings, with a large highly ornamented umbrella over each. The body was wrapped in a gold cloth, and the face covered with gold leaf. It was removed from one coffin to another in sight of our house, and in a way that quite shocked me. Eight men took it on their shoulders, and danced with it in that position, accompanied by the shouts of the multitude, and the deafening sound of native drums, tom toms, etc. One of the little disciples said, 'see, mama, it is as our Scriptures say, the road to hell is very broad and many walk in it!' He was formerly very fond of such heathen show."

"*Jan.* 19, 1832.—On our removal to Maulmain in 1830, our day-schools in Tavoy were entirely broken up; and it was not till last April, that I found myself sufficiently at leisure to attempt anything in that way again. I then opened a school, with five scholars, under the care of a respectable and intelligent Tavoy woman. We met with much encouragement, so that other schools have been since established, and our number of day-scholars is now about eighty. These, with the boarding-schools, two village schools, and about fifty persons who learn during the rainy season, in the Karen jungle, make upwards of one hundred and seventy under our instruction. The scholars in the jungle cannot of course visit us often; but a great many have come to be examined in their lessons, and we are surprised and delighted at the progress they have made."

Mrs. Boardman afterwards established more village-schools; but she was finally obliged to discontinue them, finding herself, especially during the rains, unable to exercise the necessary supervision over both teachers and pupils. She says, "The superintendence of the food and clothing of both the boarding-schools, together with the care of five day-schools, under native teachers, devolves wholly on me. My day schools are growing every week more and more interesting. We cannot, it is true, expect to see among them such progress, especially in Christianity, as our boarders make; but they are constantly gaining religious knowledge, and will grow up with comparatively correct ideas. They, with their teachers, attend worship, regularly on Lord's-day. The day-schools are entirely supported, at present, by the Honorable Company's allowance; and the civil commissioner, Mr. Maingy, appears much interested in their success."

That Mrs. Boardman was conducting Government-schools, on the plan she mentions, was owing—not to her superior tact, but her quiet, unassuming manner; which, creating no alarm by ostentatious usefulness, gave her almost unbounded power, wherever she chose to exercise it. Although she was not aware of the fact, it was at that time far from the policy of the Bengal government to allow the introduction of Christianity into their schools. There is a letter, addressed to the commissioner on the subject, a year after our present date, which, with his answer, will explain itself:

"*Tavoy*, Aug. 24, 1833.

"My Dear Sir,

"Mr. Mason has handed me for perusal, the extract from your letter to Government, which you kindly sent him. I apprehend I have hitherto had wrong impressions, in reference to the ground on which the Honourable Company patronize schools in their territories; and I hope you will allow me to say, that it would not accord with my feelings and sentiments, to banish religious instruction from the schools under my care. I think it desirable for the rising generation of this Province, to become acquainted with useful science; and the male part of the population, with the English language.

But it is infinitely more important that they receive into their hearts our holy religion, which is the source of so much happiness in this state, and imparts the hope of a glorious immortality in the world to come. Parents and guardians must know, that there is more or less danger of their children deserting the faith of their ancestors, if placed under the care of a Foreign Missionary; and the example of some of the pupils is calculated to increase such apprehensions. Mr. Boardman baptized into the Christian religion several of his scholars. One of the number is now a devoted preacher; and notwithstanding the decease of their beloved and revered teacher, they all, with one unhappy exception, remain firm in the Christian faith.

"The success of the Hindoo College, where religious instruction was interdicted, may perhaps be urged in favor of pursuing a similar course in schools here. But it strikes me, that the case is different here, even admitting *their* course to be right. The overthrow of a system so replete with cruel and impure rites, as the Hindoo, or so degrading as the Mahometan, *might* be matter of joy, though no better religion were introduced in its stead. But the Burman system of morality is superior to that of the nations around them, and to the heathen of ancient times, and is surpassed only by the divine precepts of our blessed Saviour. Like all other merely *human* institutions, it is destitute of saving power; but its influence on the people, so far as it is felt, is salutary, and their moral character will, I should think, bear a comparison with that of any heathen nation in the world. The person who should spend his days in teaching them mere human science, (though he might undermine their false tenets) by neglecting to set before them brighter hopes and purer principles, would, I imagine, live to very little purpose. For myself, sure I am, I should at last suffer the overwhelming conviction of having labored in vain.

"With this view of things, you will not, my dear sir, be surprised at my saying, it is impossible for me to pursue a course so utterly repugnant to my feelings, and so contrary to my judgment, as to banish religious instruction from the schools in my charge. It is what I am confident you yourself would not wish; but I infer from a remark in your letter that such are the terms on which Government affords patronage. It would be wrong to deceive the patrons of the schools; and if my supposition is correct, I can do no otherwise than request, that the monthly allowance be withdrawn. It will assist in establishing schools at Maulmain, on a plan more consonant with the wishes of Government than mine has ever been. Meanwhile, I trust, I shall be able to represent the claims of my pupils in such a manner, as to obtain support and countenance from those, who would wish the children to be taught the principles of the Christian faith.

"Allow me, my dear sir, to subscribe myself,

"Yours, most respectfully,

"Sarah H. Boardman."

"My Dear Madam,

"I cannot do otherwise than honor and respect the sentiments conveyed in your letter, now received. You will, I hope, give me credit for sincerity, when I assure you, that in alluding to the system of instruction pursued by you, it has ever been a source of pride to me, to point out the quiet way, in which your scholars have been made acquainted with the Christian religion. My own Government in no way proscribes the teaching of Christianity. The observations in my official letter are intended to support what I have before brought to the notice of Government, that *all* are received, who present themselves for instruction at your schools, without any stipulation as to their becoming members of the Christian faith.

I cannot express to you how much your letter has distressed me. It has been a subject of consideration with me, for some months past, how I could best succeed in establishing a college here, the scholars of which were to have been instructed on the same system, which you have so successfully pursued. Believe me,

"Yours very faithfully,

"A. D. Maingy.

"Saturday."

Mrs. Boardman's firmness, on this occasion, was advantageous to her cause; for an appropriation was afterwards obtained from Government for schools throughout the Provinces, "to be conducted on the plan of Mrs. Boardman's schools, at Tavoy." The plan was not carried out in all respects; for the propagation of Christianity in them was soon prohibited; but *she* was always allowed to teach as her own conscience dictated.

Immediately after the death of her husband, Mrs. Boardman commenced the study of the Karen, but her heavy duties prevented her from making much progress, and it was at length abandoned. She was well read in the Burmese, and was exceedingly fond of it. The following letter, addressed to the Translator of the Burmese Scriptures, will serve to give some idea of her knowledge of the language, and also of the pleasure she found in the study of the Bible in that tongue.

"*Tavoy,* Feb. 17th, 1834.

"My Dear Brother,

"The translation of the Bible into Burmese is an event, to which thousands have looked forward with joyful anticipation, and for which, thousands now perishing in their sins, should fall on their knees in thanksgiving to God, and through which, thousands yet unborn will praise him for ever and ever.

"My dear brother, I dare not pass encomiums upon a fellow-mortal in speaking of the Word of God; and if you think me guilty of this impiety in what I may say, bear with me yourself, and pray God to forgive me. I have, for the last four years, been in the daily practice of reading attentively the New-Testament in Burmese; and the more I study it, the better I am pleased and satisfied with the translation. I am delighted with the graphic style of the narrative part; and think many of the doctrinal passages are expressed with a force and perspicuity entirely wanting in our version. How much of this is due to your vivid manner of expression, and how much to the nature of the language, I do not know. I sometimes tell the Masons, that I should be willing to learn Burmese for the sake of being able to read the Scriptures in that language.

Last Lord's-day, while reading a portion of Scripture, I was affected to tears, and could scarcely proceed, as is often the case, in reading striking passages; and the effect was also observable on the old Tavoyan, for he managed to bring a great part of it into his prayer, which immediately followed. My scholars are now reading the Gospel of Luke; and I am reading St. John's Gospel and Revelation alternately, at evening worship.

"Yours affectionately,

"SARAH H. BOARDMAN."

Mrs. Boardman's tours in the Karen wilderness, with little George borne in the arms of her followers beside her—through wild, mountain passes, over swollen streams, and deceitful marshes, and among the craggy rocks and tangled shrubs of the jungle—if they could be spread out in detail, would doubtless present scenes of thrilling interest. But her singular modesty always made her silent on a subject, which would present her in a light so enterprising and adventurous. Even her most intimate friends could seldom draw from her anything on the subject; and they knew little more, than that such tours were made, and that the progress of the gospel was not suspended among the Karens, while her husband's successor was engaged in the study of the language. There is a note addressed to Mrs. Mason, from a zayat by the way-side, just before she reached the mountains; and this is the only scrap among her writings, alluding in any way to those tours. It was sent back by a party of men, who were to bring her provisions, and contains only directions about the things necessary to her journey. She says, "Perhaps you had better send the chair, as it is convenient to be carried over the streams, when they are deep. You will laugh, when I tell you, that I have forded all the smaller ones."

A single anecdote is related by Captain F——, a British officer, stationed at Tavoy; and he used to dwell with much unction on the lovely apparition, which once greeted him among those wild, dreary mountains. He had left Tavoy, accompanied by a few followers, I think on a hunting expedition, and had strolled far into the jungle. The heavy rains, which deluge this country in the summer, had not yet commenced; but they were near at hand, and during the night had sent an earnest of their coming, which was anything but agreeable. All along his path hung the dripping trailers, and beneath his feet were the roots of vegetables, half-bared, and half-imbedded in mud; while the dark clouds, with the rain almost incessantly pouring from them, and the crazy clusters of bamboo huts, which appeared here and there in the gloomy waste, and were honored by the name of village, made up a scene of desolation absolutely indescribable. A heavy shower coming up as he approached a zayat by the way-side, and far from even one of those primitive villages, he hastily took refuge beneath the roof. Here, in no very good humor with the world, especially Asiatic jungles and tropic rains, he sulkily "whistled for want of thought," and employed his eyes in watching the preparations for his breakfast.

"Uh! what wretched corners the world has, hidden beyond its oceans and behind its trees!"

Just as he had made this sage mental reflection, he was startled by the vision of a fair, smiling face in front of the zayat, the property of a dripping figure, which seemed to his surprised imagination to have stepped that moment from the clouds. But the party of wild Karen followers, which gathered round her, had a very human air; and the slight burdens they bore, spoke of human wants and human cares. The lady seemed as much surprised as himself; but she curtsied with ready grace, as she made some pleasant remark in English; and then turned to retire. Here was a dilemma. He could not suffer the lady to go out into the rain, but—his miserable accommodations, and still more miserable breakfast! He hesitated and stammered; but her quick apprehension had taken in all at a glance, and she at once relieved him from his embarrassment. Mentioning her name and errand, she added, smiling, that the emergencies of the wilderness were not new to her; and now she begged leave to put her own breakfast with his, and make up a pleasant morning party. Then beckoning to her Karens, she spoke a few unintelligible words, and disappeared under a low shed—a moldering appendage of the zayat. She soon returned with the same sunny face, and in dry clothing; and very pleasant indeed was the interview between the pious officer and the lady-missionary. They were friends afterward and the circumstances of their first meeting proved a very charming reminiscence.

Mrs. Boardman had always been peculiarly domestic in her character and habits; esteeming herself blessed above measure, when in the bosom of her family, administering to her husband's happiness, or unfolding the budding intellects of her children, and fitting their little spirits for their future destiny. But now she sat in the zayat, which had been erected for her husband, at the foot of the mountain, and in others, wherever a little company of worshippers could be collected, and performed even weightier offices, than those of Miriam and Anna; not like the wild-eyed priestess of Apollo, breathing burning words from the sacred tripod, and mad with imagined inspiration; but meek, and sometimes tearful, speaking in low, gentle accents, and with a manner sweetly persuasive. In several instances she thus conducted the worship of two or three hundred Karens, through the medium of her Burmese interpreter; and such was her modest manner of accomplishing the unusual task, that even the most fastidious were pleased; and a high officer of the English Church, which is well-known to take strict cognizance of irregularities, saw fit to bestow upon her unqualified praise. These acts, however, were not in accordance with her feminine taste or her sense of propriety. The duty, which called her to them, was fashioned by peculiar circumstances; and, as soon as opportunity offered, she gladly relinquished the task, in favor of a person better suited to its performance.

Chapter 12

A NEW HOME

"The love-lit eye, too, ere she spoke,
Forestalled the office of her tongue;
And hearts on which its radiance broke,
Thrilled with new life and heavenward sprung;
And prayer and praise, where'er she trod,
Bore witness that she walked with God."

—*Renne.*

At the commencement of the fourth year of her widowhood, Mrs. Boardman, by accepting the name of one, whom, long after, she declares to be, "a complete assemblage of all that a woman's heart could wish to love and honor," found herself in a new station, with new duties clustering thickly around her. She parted from her "beloved Karens" with the less regret, that they were left in charge of judicious and devoted "teachers." But she never forgot them, and, for many years, she required a list of all the converts to be sent her, and frequently had occasion to rejoice over the final ingathering of those, for whose salvation she had, in former times, zealously labored. Maulmain had grown into a large, populous town, since young Boardman erected his bamboo cottage in the jungle; new missionaries had gathered there; several flourishing schools had been established; and the printing-press was sending forth its publications in every direction. When she left her first Burman home, in 1828, for Tavoy, there was one church at Maulmain, containing three native members! Now, in charge of her present husband, were three flourishing churches—one Burmese, of about a hundred members, and two Karen, containing unitedly the same number. An English church had also been established by the missionaries, but was kept in a fluctuating state, by the frequent changes occurring in the army. Still this success seemed to those who occupied a position to measure the extent of the immense field, but one small step in their progress; and Mrs. Judson, instead of finding her usefulness retarded by her new position, saw opening before her a wider and more effective range. The river of her life now flowed on more evenly—deeper, broader, serener—with nothing to obstruct its course; but its wealth of waters scarce made a sound, as they floated by. It was a life of which there is much to remember, and little to tell; as, a year of stirring events may fill a volume, while perhaps the dozen valuable years of patient toil and quiet endurance that follow, have their only record on a single page. She did not establish schools, for that ground was already occupied; nor did she make long tours in the wilderness, and speak to listening crowds in the zayat; but she was in heart and life a missionary still. "I can truly say," she writes to a very intimate friend, a year after her marriage, "that the mission cause and missionary labor is increasingly dear to me, every month of my life. I am now united with one, whose heavenly spirit and example is deeply calculated to make me more devoted to the cause, than I ever have been before. Oh, that I may profit by such precious advantages."

Immediately after her arrival at Maulmain, the Civil Commissioner invited Mrs. Judson to take charge of a Government School, which was to be conducted on the same plan as those at Tavoy; but, in view of other labors, it was thought advisable for her to decline.

A large share of the population of Maulmain, and Amherst consisted of Peguans, (called by the Burmans, Talaings,) a people entirely distinct from the Burmans, in everything but religion.

About a century ago, they made war upon Burmah, and subdued the entire empire, but their star was only a short time in the ascendant. Alompra, the founder of the present dynasty in Burmah, by his combined bravery and cunning, delivered his country from its chains, and the victors became, in their turn, the vanquished. It was now the policy of the Burman government to give permanency to their success, by up-rooting the old Peguan dynasty; and the whole royal family, even in its most remote branches, was swept away. The king, a venerable, white-haired old man, was conveyed with great pomp to the capital, where he suffered an ignominious death, amid the triumphs of his enemies; and the nation was, henceforth, fairly incorporated with the Burman. The language was, at different times, proscribed; and men living in Burman towns seldom ventured to use it, except in secret. Affairs remained in this condition between the two nations, till the close of the Burmese and English war; when the Peguans, headed by an old man, more fiery than powerful, who boasted some few diluted drops of the blood-royal, made an effort to regain their freedom. When the English steamer passed down the Irrawaddy, after the treaty, the warlike demonstrations on the way produced no little surprise. Rangoon was besieged, and all the country round was swarming with rebellious Peguans. A missionary, who accompanied Commissioner Crawford on this occasion, relates many thrilling anecdotes, which, however interesting, would be irrelevant here; but perhaps the deep interest, which he afterwards exhibited in the vanquished and scattered Peguans, may have been in part founded on these circumstances. The English unwittingly gave the death-blow to the insurrection. The Peguans were in possession of the country; and the Burmese within the besieged town were suffering for lack of food, which could not be conveyed to them, while the enemy held posts along the river. As the steamer passed on her way, the firing was suspended out of respect to the British flag. The Burmans had foreseen this, and despatched boat-loads of provisions, to follow in the vessel's wake, plying the oar at night in places where they could do so with safety, while she lay at anchor, and concealing themselves during the day in the windings of the river, as near as they could follow. The *ruse* was successful; the provisions were landed at Rangoon, and the Peguans shortly after raised the siege, and fled to the English provinces for protection. Most of these people, especially the men, were in some degree familiar with the Burmese language; but it was found very difficult to give them religious instruction through this medium. After a time, a man, who had served as interpreter between his countrymen and the American teachers, was employed by one of the latter, to render a Burmese tract in his native tongue; but as there was no one to revise it, the task was doubtless very imperfectly executed. However, the old Christian woman, to whom it was first read, was almost wild with delight; and this circumstance excited an interest in behalf of the Peguans, which could not be smothered by other duties, however important. And, from this time, their language became, through one who could not himself pursue the study of it, an importunate beggar at the heart of every missionary, whose hands were not full. Mr. and Mrs. Jones looked into it a little before they finally turned to the Siamese; and then Mrs. Simons was induced to make a beginning, but she soon abandoned it for other employment. On the arrival of Mrs. Judson from Tavoy, she entered at once into her husband's views, and commenced the study of this new language, with patient assiduity; and during the three or four years which she devoted to it, she made no inconsiderable progress. She also established female prayer meetings in the church, of which her husband was pastor; having the timid Burmese women come to her in classes, instead of forming together one great assembly.

Beside this, she collected a class to whom she weekly taught the Scriptures; and under her direction, the mothers of the church formed themselves into a maternal society, "which," she says in a letter, "meets once a month, and is becoming every month more and more interesting." Then there were the seemingly-small, never-ceasing duties of a pastor's wife; the ignorant to instruct by the daily, patient "line upon line," the erring to admonish, the sorrowful to pray over, little difficulties to settle, and many a small obstacle to remove from the path that weak, timid feet were treading; "for," she says, "about half of the church are females, who require to be guided and led along like children."

Soon after Mrs. Judson's removal to Maulmain, she was again seized with the alarming malady, which had already made such inroads on her constitution. After many weeks of doubtful lingering, she began slowly to recover: but, as she attributed the perfect, uninterrupted health, which she afterwards enjoyed, to a cause within the reach of all who come to this land of shortened lives, it may be well to give the entire account, in her own words:

"When I first came up from Tavoy, I was thin and pale; and though I called myself pretty well, I had no appetite for food, and was scarce able to walk half a mile. Soon after, was called to endure a long and severe attack of illness, which brought me to the brink of the grave. I was never so low in any former illness, and the doctor who attended me, has since told me, that he had no hope of my recovery; and that when he came to prescribe medicine for me, it was more out of regard to the feelings of my husband, than from any prospect of its affording me relief. I lay confined to my bed, week after week, unable to move, except as Mr. Judson sometimes carried me in his arms from the bed to the couch for a change; and even this once brought on a return of the disease, which very nearly cost me my life. . . . I never shall forget the precious seasons enjoyed on that sick bed. Little George will tell you about it, if you should ever see him. I think he will always remember some sweet conversations I had with him, on the state of his soul, at that time. Dear child! his mind was very tender, and he would weep on account of his sins, and would kneel down and pray with all the fervor and simplicity of childhood. He used to read the Bible to me every day, and commit little hymns to memory by my bedside. . . . It pleased my Heavenly Father to raise me up again, although I was for a long time very weak. As soon as I was able, I commenced riding on horseback, and used to take a long ride every morning before sunrise. After a patient trial, I found that riding improved my health; though many times I should have become discouraged and given it up, but for the perseverance of my husband. After riding almost every day, for four or five months, I found my health so much improved, and gained strength so fast, that I began to think walking might be substituted. About this time, my nice little pony died, and we commenced a regular system of exercise on foot, walking at a rapid pace, far over the hills beyond the town, before the sun was up, every morning. We have continued this perseveringly up to the present time; and, during these years, my health has been better than at any time previous, since my arrival in India; and my constitution seems to have undergone an entire renovation."

Soon after this, the native Christians in Burmah Proper, were called to endure violent persecutions; but the commotions could not reach the provinces; and there, under the protection of the British flag, the religion of Christ was daily gaining new adherents. In one letter Mrs. Judson announces the baptism of eighteen, who were united to the Burmese church, and adds, "The Karens are flocking into the kingdom by scores." Information concerning her own occupation, during this time, must be gleaned from her letters, in fragments.

"My time is chiefly devoted to the study of the Peguan, and to the instruction of the native Christians and inquirers." "My female prayer-meetings are very interesting. Yesterday twenty-six Burman women met with me, at different times; and we had six inquirers, four of whom I think very hopeful."

"My husband is busy, early and late, superintending the publication of the Burmese Bible, and taking care of his church,"—(the Burmese;—the two Karen churches had, previous to this, been delivered to Mr. Vinton, who has since proved, not only a powerful preacher in that tongue, but one of the most zealous and persevering of laborers.) "In the midst of his multiplied duties, it is a great gratification to me that I am able to relieve him, in some measure, by giving instruction and advice to the native Christians, and settling little difficulties among them." "We have lately established a Sabbath-School, on the plan most generally adopted in America; and it promises to be successful and permanent. It embraces all the day-schools—six in number—and some members of the church beside. Mr. Osgood superintends it, and Mrs. Hancock and myself assist. It is conducted, of course, entirely in the Burmese language."

"When I last wrote you, I think I mentioned that I was revising the standard tracts in Peguan. I have finished the 'Catechism,' 'View,' 'Balance,' and 'Investigator,' and gone partly through with the Gospel of St. Luke."

"The last Peguan tract we published was the 'Ship of Grace,' which was written in Burmese by my departed husband."

Assisted by Ko Man-boke, a Peguan Christian, who was familiar with the Burmese, she followed her revision of the tracts by a translation of the New Testament; and at the close of the year 1837, she gave to the press an edition of the Life of Christ, which she had translated from the Burmese. In the meantime, Mr. Haswell had arrived; and, as soon as she could do so to advantage, she gladly placed all her books, and papers in the hands of a missionary, of whose facility in acquiring languages she speaks admiringly; and whose indefatigable labors in a field, which had interested her so deeply, must have been very gratifying.

Mrs. Judson's labors in the Peguan, were somewhat singular; indeed, I believe scarce precedented. Missionaries sometimes abandon one language and devote themselves to the acquisition of another, in which they hope to effect more good. But I know of only one other instance (Ann H. Judson, in the Siamese) of stepping from the path which has grown familiar to the foot, toiling for years merely to supply an exigency, and then, resigning the labor and its fruits to another, as willingly as though it had never cost an effort. She used to sit by her study-table, all day long, except when called elsewhere by imperative duty, with two or three assistants about her; and, though the translations and revisions there made were necessarily imperfect, there has been a time when they were invaluable.

It was from this position, that the following words were penned: "I am sure, my dear parents, that you have never regretted giving up your beloved child, your first-born, to the cause of Christ. However unworthy the offering, it was valuable to you; and if given up in a right spirit, it has been the source of most precious blessings to your souls. It is in this state of existence only, that we can testify our gratitude to the Saviour, by suffering and denying ourselves for him. Oh! as we draw near eternity, and the bubbles of earth recede from our dazzled vision, shall we not lament that we have done so little for Christ—that we have been willing to deny ourselves so little for His sake who gave up his life for us? Oh! let us live for the Saviour, and then, after a long separation on earth, how sweet to meet at God's right hand, to part no more for ever!"

The letter continues, "The little ones play in the verandah, adjoining the room where I sit all the day, with my Peguan translator. It is open to the road, and I often have inquirers. Since I commenced this letter, I happened to look up, and saw a man leaning over the balustrade, looking at me very attentively. The thought occurred to me, he may be one of the dear *chosen ones*, and may have been guided to this place to hear the blessed Gospel. So I asked him what he wanted. He replied, he was looking to see me write. I immediately laid down my pen, invited him in, and he sat a long time listening to the truth. He promised to pray to the Eternal God, to give him a new heart, that he might believe in the Saviour, the Lord Jesus Christ, of whom he says he never heard till today. He is a Shan, who has been residing for a number of years at Pegu, and came here for trade. He lives in his boat; and, while strolling about the streets, was led by curiosity hither; and oh, may it be for the salvation of his soul!"

This manner of life, as has been before intimated, had no showiness about it; but every moment of time—each golden sand, as it dropped from the glass, combined with that which went before, to be molded into jewels of infinite richness. Notwithstanding the bright promise of Mrs. Judson's girlhood, her intellect was in reality not a precocious one, and there had been no premature development. On the contrary, every day in her new position, gave strength and compass to her mental powers, and increased loftiness to her character, without abating its attractive gentleness. So, even in this life, begin "the children of light" to mount the ladder, whose gradations will be the measure of eternity.

Chapter 13

THE MOTHER AND CHILD

"He's gone, but oft in memory's light,
His cherished face will shine,
His plaintive voice be in my ear,
His little hand in mine."

—*Judson.*

We have passed one event in Mrs. Judson's life—the greatest of all trials which beset, a missionary's trial-lined path—without mention. It is a hard thing for a mother to lay the child of her love, from her bosom, to the dark, damp pillow fashioned by the sexton's spade; it is very hard; but when the little spirit passes from the clay, both hope and fear pass with it, and even love lies down to a sleep of beautiful dreams, to awake at last with its renovated treasure in Paradise. She knows that her precious lamb is folded in the Saviour's arms; and sorrow gathers a serene sweetness, more grateful to a meek heart than the brightest phase of joy. Not thus does the mother think upon the living child, that she has exiled from her bosom, though it may have been in her power to provide for it a pillow of roses. Both hope and fear assume a painful intensity, which time never softens; and love is not only awake and watchful, but its keen-sightedness fashions many an ill, which has no existence in reality. This sacrifice is not peculiar to the missionary. The Anglo-Saxon blood seems to degenerate under the influence of an Asiatic sun; and the child must be sent away to develop under more favorable circumstances, or arrive at manhood, crippled in mind and muscle; and in this enfeebled state, (if he have not already commenced the sad career) run the gauntlet of almost every vice. But there is one great difference. Most Europeans are but temporary residents in India. The missionary alone watches the ship, as it bears away his treasure, with scarce the shadow of a hope that he will ever look upon the beloved face again on earth. He may watch over its welfare from a distance, he may lay plans, and make sacrifices, and advise, and pray; he may still be the guiding-star of its existence; but all the sweet cares, the fond solicitude which has its origin in daily watching, the tenderer and more beautiful duties of the parent, are transferred for ever to another.

Mrs. Judson had taken the formidable resolution of parting with her one darling boy, previous to her second marriage; and soon after this event, an opportunity offered for sending him to America, which might not occur again in many years. The ship Cashmere had brought a number of Missionaries to Maulmain; and would return directly to Boston, with the exception of a few weeks to be passed at Singapore. Mrs. Judson hesitated, for little George, being her "only one," had been most tenderly nurtured; and his nature had about it a clinging tenderness and sensitiveness, which peculiarly unfitted him for contact with strangers. Would he not read cruelty, instead of carelessness, in their cold eyes? And would not the voices, which love did not modulate, sound harsh to him? Oh, how his little heart *must* sometimes ache, when there would be none to comfort him! If he could only be under a woman's care, though it were not her own!—but no; she must confide him to men, young men, who, however kind might be their intentions, could never look into the spirit of her little boy and mark its delicate workings, or comprehend, in the slightest degree, the feeling agitating her own bosom. Yet they promised, and spoke kindly and feelingly; and—the decisive argument—this was her only opportunity. And so she says, "After deliberation, accompanied with tears and agony and prayers, I came to the conviction that it was my duty to send away my only child, my darling George, and yesterday he bade me a long farewell. Oh, my dear sister! my heart is full, and I long to disburden it by writing you whole pages: but my eyes are rolling down with tears, and I can scarcely hold my pen." . . . "Oh! I shall never forget his looks, as he stood by the door and gazed at me for the last time. His eyes were filling with tears, and his little face red with suppressed emotion. But he subdued his feelings, and it was not till he had turned away, and was going down the steps that he burst into a flood of tears. I hurried to my room; and on my knees, with my whole heart, gave him up to God; and my bursting heart was comforted from above. I felt such a love to poor perishing souls, as made me willing to give up all, that I might aid in the work of bringing these wretched heathen to Christ. The love of God, manifested in sending his only-begotten and well beloved Son into this world, to die for *our* sins, touched my heart, and I felt satisfaction in laying upon the altar my only son. My reason and judgment tell me that the good of my child requires that he should be sent to America; and this, of itself, would support me in some little degree; but when I view it as a *sacrifice*, made for the sake of Jesus, it becomes a *delightful privilege*. I feel a great degree of confidence, that George will be converted, and I cannot but hope he will one day return to Burmah, a missionary of the Cross, as his dear father was. . . . His dear papa took him down to Amherst in a boat. He held him in his arms all the way; and he says his conversation was very affectionate and intelligent. He saw his little bed prepared in the cabin, and everything as comfortable and pleasant as possible, and then, as Georgie expressed it, returned to 'comfort mama.' And much did I need comfort; for this is, in some respects, the severest trial I have ever met with."

Here let us leave the mother to her griefs and consolations; and give, here and there, a glance at the little wanderer, who has commenced the long dreary voyage, to the land of his parents' birth. We find him at first, surrounded by gentle and loving friends—so gentle, and so loving, that he scarce misses his mother's voice and kiss; and longs to behold her only, that he may give her an account of the wonders he is from day to day beholding. Every body loves him, and studies his happiness. The missionaries destined to Singapore pity him, and pity the parents left behind, and they vie with each other in bestowing upon him the minutest attention which they think might be suggested by a mother's love. The officers and the crew are all charmed with him; for the presence of a child in the ship is not a common thing, and he is a child of peculiar gentleness. Arrived at Singapore, he is still with missionaries, whose sympathies are all enlisted in his behalf; and their children are his pleasant playmates. And now he attracts other attention; and so he goes to sit in richly furnished apartments, such as he has never seen before; and he looks at handsome paintings, and walks through fine gardens, while he is loaded with caresses by those who wonder of what magic power the mother is possessed, who has thus far, and thus well, bred up her son in heathen Burmah.

Next, we will step into the open boat, and follow the little wanderer to the ship all ready to spread her sails for America. It is rowed by natives; but the child is still under the protection of the two missionaries, Jones and Dean. They are ten miles from the shore, and five from the ship—all alone, and without arms. A boat with three wild, fierce-looking men, hails them in a seeming friendly manner; and, coming near enough to spy out their strength, or rather weakness, moves on. But the little company suspects no danger. A few moments pass, and the spy-boat re-appears. It heads directly towards them, and comes with more speed—a sail hoisted, and better manned. A quick glance of suspicion is exchanged, but there is time for no more, for the sail is close alongside. The strangers ask but a cluster of fruit, however, and one of the gentlemen rises to give it them. What a gleaming of fiendish eyes! A moment of rapid action succeeds—a push—a plunge—and the kind fruit-giver is struggling with the waves which have closed above his head. They attempt to wrestle a little with his companion, but finally seize their arms.

The little boy, from his hiding-place beneath a bench, marks every thrust; and his flesh creeps, and his blue eyes glitter and dilate until they assume an intense blackness. And now the form of his protector sways and reels, and the red blood trickles from his wounded side to the bottom of the boat. He stands, however, and receives another wound. And now the three iron prongs of a fishing spear send their barbed points through bone and muscle, and the heavy wooden handle is left hanging from the transfixed and bleeding wrist. At this fearful crisis, a hand from without clutches the boat—a pale, dripping face appears, and the drowning man is dragged over the side, by the bewildered oarsman. What a place to seek safety in! The marauders stand with drawn cutlass, or brandishing the curved creese; but they pause a moment in their deadly work, and substitute threats for blows. Their tones are those of infuriated madmen, and their gestures—hah! a light begins to break? Can that one small box, standing so unpretendingly in the centre of the boat, be the cause of the affray? It contains treasure, true, but not such as they can appreciate—messages of love from absent children, brothers, sisters and friends, to those who would value them far above gold and rubies. It is gladly flung to them, however, and the pirate-boat wheels and flees, like a bird of prey.

Thank God, that death came neither in the wave nor the steel! And oh, how heart-felt, how unutterably deep, will be the mother's gratitude, when she hears of her darling's safety! When she knows that he has not been borne away to some dark haunt of vice and crime, to be bred to the bloody trade of a wild Malayan corsair!

We might follow the little child still farther. We might see him stand, with paled cheek, and lip quivering, watching the death-agonies of the pet-goat, which had been his playmate in the green compound at Maulmain, while it occurred to none of the sailors who stood laughing by, to explain to him the reason, (if reason there was) for the seemingly wanton deed. We might see him, who, from necessity, had been the constant companion of a quiet, refined, delicate mother, and whose little spirit was all too sensitively attuned, shrinking, shocked and frightened, from the coarse, rude jests, which were intended for his amusement; and regarding the blunt kindness, which esteemed itself all sufficient to "make a man of him," as the bitterest cruelty. We might mark his lonely pillow wetted by his tears at night, and in the day, see him creep away alone to the boat, suspended at the stern of the ship, and gaze far over the blue waters till his eyes were too dim to discern their line of meeting with the horizon; and then lean his face upon his knees, and relieve his childish misery by unchecked sobbings. But the mother followed him only in imagination—not in *spirit*, for God, in mercy, denies to mortals that communion by which the chords of her heart would now have been stirred so agonizingly. She had committed her treasure to a true Friend; and she knew that in sickness or in health, in the ship or beneath the wave, he rested in the hollow of an Omnipotent Hand, and the wing of peace was over him.

Soon after the separation, George received a little copy of verses from his mother, which I wish I could place upon the page, as it lies before me now—the large letters carefully printed by her pen, that he might be able to read it without assistance; and the nice paper lining afterwards stitched around by the fingers of the grateful son. A high degree of literary or poetic merit would not be considered indispensable to such a production, unless it were addressed to an ideal instead of a real child, or intended for more than one little pair of eyes; but as the verses possess at least the merit of appropriateness, I will venture to write them down without their attractive concomitants.

FOR MY DARLING GEORGIE.

"You cannot see your dear mama,
But think of her, my love;
Nor can you see your dear papa,
For he's in heaven above.

Your sister Sarah, too, is gone,
And little brother dear;—
But still, my child, you're not alone.
For God is ever near."

Something of Mrs. Judson's character, as a mother, and her mode of instruction, may be inferred from the following letter to her little son:

"*Maulmain*, May 5th, 1835.
"My Darling Child,

"Your papa has today received a letter from Mr. Dean, informing us that Mrs. Dean has gone to heaven—that happy world, where your own dear father, and your little brother and sister have been for several years—that blessed world, where Jesus is who died on the cross for our sins, and who rose from the dead on the third day—that blessed world where there is no more sorrow, or sin, or separation, or death. Do you sometimes weep and feel very sorry because you cannot see your mama? Your mama also feels very sad, and weeps sometimes, because she cannot live with her dear, only little boy. But, Georgie, if we are so blessed as to reach heaven when we die, we shall never be parted again, and shall never weep any more.

"Mr. Dean writes, that you are a good boy, and it makes your dear papa and myself very happy to hear so. If you are really and truly a good boy, if you are afraid to sin, afraid to do any thing that God will not approve, though unknown to your friends, Jesus will love you and bless you. Some little boys appear to be very good and obedient, in the presence of their parents, or persons older than themselves, but when alone, or with other children, they think naughty thoughts, say naughty words, and do naughty things. Because they behave well in the presence of their parents and teachers, their friends think they are very good. But they are not good, and God does not love such naughty little boys; and if their papas and mamas knew that their children were naughty out of their sight, they would be very unhappy. Remember, my dear child, that *God sees you at all times.*

"Do you know, George, the meaning of the word *deceive?* I will try to explain it to you. Once at evening worship, in the Burman Chapel, you did not kneel down at prayer, but just as your papa was going to say 'amen,' you got down softly from your chair and knelt a moment, so that you might rise while the rest of the people were rising. Now consider—what did you kneel down and get up immediately for? It was, that we might think you had been kneeling all prayer-time. And yet you had not been kneeling all prayer time—only a moment. This is what we mean by *deceiving*—making others think a thing different from what it really is.

"I will tell you, my dear child, several ways in which it would have been proper for you to act at the native worship. One is this: You might have knelt down at first, and when you found yourself growing tired, you might have kept thinking in your mind, 'true, I am very tired, and my knees ache very much, but I will try to keep still and think of praying to God, till prayer is over.' Or, if you were too sleepy to think, you might have got up and sat in your chair, till prayer was done, and after worship, said, 'Dear papa, I was too tired and sleepy to kneel down at prayers this evening—please excuse me.' You should not have tried to make us think you knelt, when you did not, because that is *deceiving*. You were then a very little boy, and did not know any better. Whenever you do anything wrong now, my darling, go immediately and confess it to your friends, and ask them to forgive you; and pray God to forgive you.

"Your papa sends much love. He wrote you a little while ago; and sent some pretty lines, which he composed himself, for you to learn. He says that you were an obedient, affectionate child, when with us; and he prays that you may become a Christian.

"Don't lose this letter, Georgie, for it has some things in it which I wish you to remember. Keep it folded in a piece of paper to read again; and if you cannot understand it all, ask some kind friend to explain it to you.

"Farewell. God bless you, my dear, dear child!

"Your affectionate mama,

"Sarah Judson."

It is a matter of regret that the long letter, which accompanied little George to his future guardians, is not in our possession; for it would doubtless unfold a system of maternal management, which, in his own case, and that of the children who succeeded him, has been singularly successful. But if it be still in existence, its possessor is not known; and we must content ourselves with a few extracts from a letter of a more general character, addressed to the lady who was to find her child a home. After speaking of some slight tendency to the fatal *cough*, which she had so much reason to dread, in connection with a residence in a northern climate, and giving some prescriptions for it, she adds particulars about clothing, food, exercise, etc. etc., which, shows that in the mental and moral training of her child, she was far from neglecting his physical development. "Let George," she continues, "call the persons, with whom he finds a home, 'uncle' and 'aunt,' if they desire it, but I do not like to have him call others 'papa' and 'mama' while we live. Let him often be reminded of us; and let the love which he now feels for us be carefully cherished. I could not bear to be forgotten by the little one, who was so long my only earthly comfort." Then she mentions some necessary qualifications of those, who take charge of her little son. They must be "conscientious and pious—a family over whom religion, practical and heartfelt religion, maintains a constant influence. Oh! may he fall into the hands of persons, who will watch vigilantly over him, and detect and check the first developments of the natural heart; persons who desire above all things, that their children become pious, and whose daily walk and conversation be such as a little immortal may safely imitate. But, alas! who can have for my poor child the feelings of a mother? Whose heart can be so tenderly alive to every development of his little mind? Who will retire to weep and pray, as I have done, when there is danger of swerving from the right path? But I must not distrust my Heavenly Father. I have committed my child to his keeping; and I pray daily that his steps may be guided and directed from above. . . . Separated as Georgie is from me, I feel anxious to hear all about him that I can; and wish you would furnish the lady who is to take charge of him with a small blank-book, to keep a journal of his health, conduct, studies, etc., etc. I feel particularly positive on this point, and cannot be denied. Do not, I entreat you, place him with any person, who will not keep such a journal, writing it at least as often as once a week, and forward the books to me by every opportunity. I do not hesitate to say, that a person, who could refuse or neglect this, ought not to have the care of my little boy. It would operate as a strong incentive to good conduct on the part of the child, to know that a faithful account of all his actions was to be sent to his mother;—but still it is better to make the love and fear of God the great motive by which he is influenced."

The editress of the Mother's Journal remarks, in her Obituary Notice, that Mrs. Judson's friends in America were afraid to take charge of little George; "for so perfect had been his mother's work in training him thus far, that they should fear they would only mar what had been done." Mrs. Ballister, the wife of the American Consul at Singapore, became very fond of him, and expressed the greatest astonishment, that a child born, and thus far bred, in an Asiatic country, could have made such progress in mind, manners, and morals; and the friends who had charge of him, wrote from the same place, "He causes us no trouble, since he only needs to understand what we wish of him, and he is ready to do it."

Notwithstanding all this, Mrs. Judson wrote to a friend, some years later, and when she had other children about her, "I think I made one mistake in the management of George; but I trust the effect has been obviated by his being so early thrown, in some degree, upon his own resources. I allowed him to lean too much on others, instead of studying to strengthen his character, as I now see would have been better. I shall endeavour to teach my other children more independence."

We cannot do better here than add short extracts from a couple of letters, written many years afterward, when the mother's earnest prayers had been answered, and her faith had received the richest of all rewards:

"My Beloved George—The last letter which I received from America respecting you, rejoiced my heart more than the reception of any letter before in my life. It was from Doct. Bolles, and contained the joyful intelligence of your hopeful conversion to God. Still I am not fully satisfied—I am longing to hear that you 'daily grow in grace and in the knowledge of our Lord and Saviour Jesus Christ.'"

"This is the fifteenth anniversary of your birthday; and I feel it to be—I had almost said, *the* most important period in your life. At least it is very, very important, as on the turn which you now take, your course through life will probably depend. Oh, how comforting to my anxious heart is the thought, that you have decided on the most momentous of all subjects, and that you have decided right; that you have determined to identify yourself with the people of God, by leading the life of a humble follower of the blessed Jesus. Oh, how full of anguish would my soul be, now that you have arrived at this age, had I not a hope, that you were a Christian! Blessed be God! I have this sweet, this cheering, this most consoling of all hopes, to sustain my heart when ready to sink, as it measures the distance between us, or looks back upon my long separation from you, my darling, eldest son. Tears come to my eyes, and I am ready to throw aside my pen, and obey the strong impulse to weep, as I think of the endearments of your infancy, and the sweetness of your childhood, when your soft cheek was pressed to mine, and all your little griefs buried and forgotten in my bosom. I always think of you as the little, innocent, prattling boy you then were. I would fain ever think of you as such; but the picture must change; and I must try to imagine you growing up to be a tall, young man.

"I said before, that it is an unspeakable joy to my heart that you are hopefully pious. Still, I am far from being free from anxiety on your account. There is, you know, a *possibility* of our being deceived. And even if we are able to say, as we doubtless may be, 'I *know* that I have passed from death unto life,'—yet the Christian's path is beset with snares and dangers. No doubt you have already had severe struggles with remaining sin in your heart. I feel strong and peculiar desires, that you become a truly *conscientious, prayerful, devoted* Christian. Be not contented with possessing a mere hope in Christ, that He will pardon your sins and save you at last. Live with religion in daily exercise in your soul. Then you will—you *must* be happy. Can you resolve to devote your whole life to the service of your blessed Saviour? Do you really give Him your heart, and determine, (with His assistance, which He will surely grant in answer to prayer) never to *do*, nor *say*, nor *think* anything contrary to His holy will? True religion, always in exercise, affords the only certain retreat from the sorrows, and trials, and sins of this mortal state.

'Draw nigh unto God, and he will draw nigh unto you.'
'Pray without ceasing.'
'Watch unto prayer.'

Chapter 14

TRIAL ON TRIAL

> "Oh! who could bear life's stormy doom,
> Did not Thy wing of love
> Come brightly wafting through the gloom,
> Our peace-branch from above?"
>
> —*Moore.*

In less than half-a-dozen years after her second marriage, Mrs. Judson thus wrote to her parents: "My beloved husband has been troubled with a cough for about six months; and, unless speedily removed, it must terminate in pulmonary consumption. It seems to me, that it would be pleasant to die with him, but oh! how could I live without him? I have already passed through many trying scenes; but now, were it not for the sure promise, 'As thy day is, so shall thy strength be,' I should yield to utter despondency, at the sad prospect before me."

Of all destroyers, she had reason to dread this the most; and now it was standing a second time on her threshold. There was the ominous cough, the shortened breath, and the pain in the side—all familiar things to her; then followed an entire failure of voice, and a consequent suspension of pastoral duties; and finally books of study were abandoned, and a sea-voyage became the last resort.

There is nothing on earth so beautiful, as the household on which love forever smiles, and where religion walks, a counsellor and friend. No cloud can darken it, for its twin-stars are centred in the soul; no storm can make it tremble—it has an earthly support, the gift of Heaven, and a heavenly anchor. But the roof beneath which it dwells shelters a sacred spot, where the curious eye must not peer, nor the stranger-foot tread. So is it with the warm, soul-breathing missives now beside me. I would fain copy enough of them, to show how the one flower, which seems to have been spared us from the wreck of Eden, gathered sweetness, when shadowed by the Cross; but my pen shrinks from desecrating their beauty. At this moment, however, a pair of young, dark eyes rise before me, that will read the page with the interest of an only and beloved daughter, and then turn back tearfully to the sad, sweet scenes, which she cannot yet have entirely forgotten. For her sake, shall a few passages be written down, that may, perhaps, recall lost fragments of the picture now in her heart.

"As soon as you left the house, I ran to your dressing-room, and watched you from the window. But you did not look up—oh, how I wished you would! Then I hastened to the back verandah, and caught one last glimpse of you through the trees; . . . and I gave vent to my feelings in a flood of tears.

"Then the children came around me, asking to go to the wharf, and the women *looked* their wishes; and though I said 'no,' to the little ones, I could not deny the others. After they were gone, I took all three of our darlings into your own little room, told them why you had gone away, and asked Abby Ann and Adoniram, if they wished me to ask God to take care of papa, while he was gone. They said 'yes;' and so I put Elnathan down on the floor to play, and, kneeling beside the other two, committed you and ourselves to the care of our Heavenly Father." After mentioning the return of the Burman women from the wharf, she speaks of other prayers; and in this connection, adds, "I never heard more appropriate petitions from the native Christians. They prayed for you, for me, and for the children, in just such a manner as I wished them to pray. Mah Hlah and Mah Tee could scarce proceed for sobs and tears.

Oh! who would not prefer the sincere, disinterested love of these simple, warm-hearted Christians, to all the applause and adulation of the world, or even to the more refined, but too often selfish regard of our equals in mental cultivation and religious knowledge! Ko Manboke says, he has only one request to make, and that is, if you must die, he begs you will come back to Maulmain, and die in the midst of the disciples, who love you so dearly."

"How sweet is the thought that, when you go into the presence of God, you always pray for me, and for our dear children! We have family worship mornings, in the sleeping-room. Abby and Pwen[1] kneel, one on each side of me, and after I have read and prayed I teach them the Lord's prayer. I make them repeat it distinctly, only two or three words at a time. They both sit at the table with me, Pwen occupying his beloved father's place. But these things do not beguile my loneliness. Oh, when shall I see you again, here, in your old seat?"

"Your little daughter and I have been praying for you this evening. She is now in bed, and I am sitting by my study-table, where I spend all my time after evening worship, except what is devoted to the children. I wish, my love, that you would pray for one object in particular—that I may be assisted in communicating divine truth to the minds of these little immortals. . . . At times the sweet hope that you will soon return, restored to perfect health, buoys up my spirit; but perhaps you will find it necessary to go farther, a necessity from which I cannot but shrink with doubt and dread; or you may come back only to die with me. This last agonizing thought crushes me down in overwhelming sorrow. I hope I do not feel unwilling, that our Heavenly Father should do as He thinks best with us; but my heart shrinks from the prospect of living in this sinful, dark, friendless world, without you. But I feel that I do wrong to anticipate sorrows. God has promised strength only for *today;* and, in infinite mercy, He shuts the future from our view. I know that there is small ground for hope—few ever recover from your disease; but it may

1 *Pwen*, a flower. A name given to Adoniram by the natives.

be, that God will restore you to health, for the sake of His suffering cause. *I* do not deserve it; and I have often wondered that I should have been so singularly blessed, as to possess that heart, which is far more precious than all the world beside. But the most satisfactory view of our condition is to look away to that blissful world, where separations are unknown. There, my beloved Judson, *we* shall surely meet each other; and we shall also meet those loved ones, who have gone before us to that haven of rest."

"After worship at the chapel, several of the native Christians came in; and we all mingled our tears together. They each in turn committed their absent pastor (father, they called you) to God, and prayed for your restoration to health, and speedy return to us, with a fervor, which I felt at the time must prevail."

And so it did. The husband, father, and pastor returned from his long absence, much improved in health; so much so, that before the close of the year, Mrs. Judson thus speaks of him to her American friends: "My husband preached on the last four Lord's-days; and oh, how happy I am to be able to say that he has received no material injury from thus using his voice. After months of anxiety, how delightful to find cause to hope that his life will be spared for many years, to bless his family and the poor, perishing Burmans."

This year was so much broken by the cares and anxieties, growing out of her husband's illness, that she could scarce be expected to follow her literary pursuits to the same advantage as formerly; but yet they were by no means neglected. She commenced a translation of Bunyan's Pilgrim's Progress; and in November she says, "I am now engaged in writing questions on the Acts of the Apostles, in Burmese, for the use of Bible Classes and Sabbath Schools. We have a Sabbath School, numbering nearly a hundred children, and a Bible Class of twenty adults."

In another letter she says, "My little family occupies nearly all my time; and if I have a leisure hour, now and then, I feel that it ought to be devoted to the instruction of the ignorant native Christians, or the still more ignorant and degraded heathen."

The same willingness to take the place in her Master's vineyard—pointed out by his finger, which influenced her in the study of the Peguan, was manifest through life. In the savage haunts of the Karen wilderness, with listening hundreds at her feet, or teaching the infant-lisper on her knee to raise its little heart to heaven—poring over her books till hand and head both ached from weariness, or whispering the magic words, which could cheer her husband's heart in the midst of his toilsome labors—teaching, counselling, and praying, surrounded by dusky faces and darker natures, or turning to the simplest and commonest domestic duty—to her, it was all the same. "Whatever her hand found to do" was done earnestly, and with ready will. There is many a fashionable English lady, from whose heart her words cannot depart, till the heart has ceased its beatings; and her missionary sisters will long remember the low pleadings of her voice, in the social prayer-meeting, and the maternal gatherings instituted for themselves and their children. It was for a meeting of this kind, that the following sweet hymn, which afterwards appeared in the Mother's Journal, was written:

MOTHER'S LITANY.

"Lamb of God, enthroned on high,
Look on us with pitying eye,
While we raise our earnest cry,
For our babes, to thee.

Once thy followers infants spurned,
But thy bosom o'er them yearned,
Nor from Canaan's daughter turned
Thy all-pitying eye.

Thou did'st give *our* spirits rest,
When with sin and grief oppressed,
In thy gentle, loving breast—
Shelter, then, our babes.

Breath divine they breathe, and wear
God's own image; yet they bear
Sin and guilt, a fearful share,—
Pity them, we pray.

Guide and guard them here below,
As through dangerous paths they go,—
Be their joy 'mid earthly woe,
Thou, their Heavenly Friend.

When, to call thy children home,
Robed in glory, thou shalt come,
For these little ones make room,
Lamb of God, we pray."

About the middle of the ensuing year, the children, now four in number, were seized with the whooping-cough, from which they suffered three or four months; and before they entirely recovered three of them were attacked by the disease of the bowels, so alarming in a tropical climate. During these troubles, the mother was suddenly prostrated; and, so low was she brought, that her friends expected momentarily to see her close her eyes in her last sleep. She afterward says, "The dear sisters of the mission came to give me a last look and pressure of the hand, for I was too far gone to speak. The poor children, three of whom were ill, were sent away; and my husband devoted his whole time to taking care of me. I felt sure that my hour of release from this world had come—that my Master was calling me; and blessed be God! I was entirely willing to leave all, and go to him."

As soon as she had gained strength enough to be removed, she was invited to take up her residence, in the family of Capt. Impey, an English officer, who was passing the hot season on the sea-shore at Amherst. The invitation, which included her children, was gratefully accepted, and she left home, taking with her the three little ones that were ill. For a time all seemed to be gradually improving; but she was finally attacked with cold, followed by fever; and at the end of the season, both herself and children returned to Maulmain, in a worse condition than they left it. The physicians now pronounced the mother and two elder children to be in imminent danger, and recommended a sea-voyage, as affording the only hope of recovery. The whole family accordingly took passage in a vessel bound for Calcutta; but by this time the Southwest Monsoon was raging, and the voyage, although as pleasant as circumstances would admit, was tempestuous, and for invalids, exceedingly uncomfortable.

"We had been out only four days," says Mrs. Judson, "when we struck on shoals, and for about twenty minutes were expecting to see the large, beautiful vessel a wreck; and then all on board must perish, or at best take refuge in a small boat, exposed to the dreary tempests. I shall never forget my feelings, as I looked over the side of the vessel that night, on the dark ocean, and fancied ourselves with our poor sick, and almost dying children, launched on its stormy waves. The captain tacked as soon as possible, and the tide rising at the time, we were providentially delivered from our extreme peril." During this scene Mrs. Judson evinced her characteristic thoughtfulness and presence of mind; for while confusion reigned throughout the ship, she crept from her berth, and with her own weak hand, filled a small trunk with articles which would be necessary, if they were driven to take refuge in the boat.

On reaching their destination, it was thought advisable to take a house at Serampore, in preference to Calcutta; but even here she says, "The weather was very unfavorable. At one time it was so oppressively hot, that we could scarcely breathe, and the next hour the cold, bleak winds would come whistling in, at the high windows, completely chilling the poor little invalids." These circumstances were certainly far from favorable to recovery, and medical advisers urged the necessity of putting to sea again. Inquiries were accordingly made concerning vessels bound for the Isle of France, but they were at first very unsatisfactory. Mrs. Judson continues her narrative: "That same day, Captain Hamlin, of the ship Ramsay, called to see us. He was a pious man, whom we had before seen; and though he had not the slightest intimation of our wish to go to the Mauritius, he offered us a passage to that place, and thence to Maulmain. His ship was to sail in ten days." Still, in consideration of the length of the voyage, the time it would consume, and its tediousness during the stormy season, they hesitated; but only for a short time. "Dear little Enna" (Elnathan) "had an alarming relapse, and Pwen and Abby were growing worse daily. Henry's symptoms appeared more favorable; but I was extremely weak, and finally, in addition to all the rest, I was again attacked with my old complaint. You may fancy, in some degree, what a fatiguing time my poor husband must have had, watching over us all, night and day." These circumstances did not admit of unnecessary delay. The ship was on the point of sailing; and Mrs. Judson, with her first slight accession of strength, was obliged to hasten to Calcutta, to make some preparations, which required her personal superintendence. She continues:—"Accordingly on the morning of the 23rd, I went with the two older children, Abby and Pwen, on board the boat. Henry was as well as he had been for weeks, and we had never thought him dangerous. As for Elnathan, we considered him almost well. While in Calcutta, the two children with me grew worse; Pwen, in addition to his previous illness, being seized with a fever, which I feared would prove fatal. I engaged a skilful surgeon, and he soon succeeded in reducing the fever; but he gave me little encouragement in either of their cases. He said a sea-voyage was their only chance, and if we could manage to keep Pwen from *getting worse*, until the ship should sail, it was the utmost we could expect.

During these trials, I heard from Serampore every day, and the accounts were for some time favorable. But on the morning of the 29th, my husband's note, dated the day before, said that Henry was not so well, and that Elnathan was ill of fever, apparently from having taken sudden cold. I determined to leave, at once, for Serampore; but on inquiry, I ascertained, that the tide would not turn till six o'clock in the evening. My friends begged me to wait till the next morning, but I could not listen to their entreaties, though I apprehended no real danger in the cases of my absent little ones. At sunset, I put Abby and Pwen to bed inside the boat, and took my dreary watch outside. Oh, what a long and desolate night that was to me! It was at the neap tides; and for the last four or five miles the men were unable to row, but pushed the boat up the stream with long bamboos. The moon was setting, and I shall never forget the melancholy feelings which crept over me, while I watched the long shadows of the trees on the darkening waters. My anxiety was heightened by hearing poor Pwen cough frequently, as though he had taken cold. The fear, that the children might be injured by their exposure, induced me to oppose every proposition to anchor, and also to urge the boatmen onward by every means in my power. At two o'clock we reached home. My dear husband met me at the door, and as he embraced me, said, 'Oh, my love, you have come to the house of death!'

'What!—oh, what is it?'

'Dear little Henry is dying.'

I flew to him, but oh, how changed! I had left him a bright little boy, running about the floor, with cheeks far from having lost their plumpness. Now, his eyes were dim, his cheek colorless, and his little form so emaciated, that, in the sincerity of my heart, I involuntarily exclaimed, Can this be Henry! Still I was relieved to find, that he was not actually in the agonies of the death-struggle. He appeared so intelligent, that I still had hope.

'Drink! drink!' he called out.

I prepared him a little wine and water, and was pleased to find that his stomach did not reject it, as it had rejected everything during the last twenty-four hours, whether food or medicine. But when I beheld his countenance by the light of day, in the morning, I saw that he could not live. During all this time, poor Elnathan was lying in a violent fever, with his head shaved, and a plaster on his chest. Truly, my dear sister, we felt that the hand of God was heavy upon us. But we bowed to His will, not daring to murmur. In the forenoon, while lying in his swing-cot, Henry looked at me most affectionately, and stretched out his little hands for me to take him. Oh, how glad I was that I came up that night! If I had waited till the next day, he would not have recognized me." During the day, the little sufferer endured violent convulsions, but he lingered on till evening. She continues, "I had my cot placed so that my head was close to his; and as I had been up all the night previous, and was still far from well, I soon fell asleep Mr. Judson sat watching him, on the other side. The first that I heard was a soft whisper, 'Henry, my dear son Henry!' The dear little creature opened his eyes, and looked into his papa's face, with all the intelligence and earnestness he was wont in days of health. But suddenly his countenance changed—his papa spoke to me—I looked at him—there was one gasp, and then all was over. The body had ceased from suffering—the spirit was at rest in the bosom of Jesus."

Both parents had seen much of sorrow before, but it is crime, not sorrow, that renders the bosom callous; and the existence of the past did not blunt the sharp point of present anguish. And even now, the survivor, who has buried his dead at Rangoon, Amherst, Maulmain, and St. Helena, has many a sweet, mournful remembrance to give to "little Henry of Serampore."

"He sleeps," says the mother, "in the Mission burial-ground, where molders the dust of Carey, Marshman, and Ward. We buried him at evening; and, while weeping at the grave, I scarcely knew whether my tears fell faster for Henry or Elnathan.

"Three days after, we left Calcutta, and on the 16th, went on board the Ramsay." The Monsoon was drawing to a close, and the storms were more dangerous than during the months previous. Frequent tempests, too sudden to allow of preparation, placed them in great peril. Under date of Sept. 4th, Mrs. Judson continues her letter:—"Could you now look on our dismasted vessel you would indeed say, she is a ship in distress. For the last three days, we have had the most frightful squalls I ever experienced; and yesterday two top-masts, a top-gallant mast, and the jib-boom, with all their sails, were torn away, causing a tremendous crash. For the two last nights, I have not closed my eyes to sleep, and I find it quite impossible to sleep now. I have, therefore, taken my pen, though the vessel rolls so, that I fear my writing will be quite illegible. Do not infer from anything I have said, that I am suffering from terror; my wakefulness has been occasioned only by bodily discomfort, arising from the violent tossing of the vessel. I thank God, that I feel perfectly calm and resigned; and I can leave myself and my dear family in His hands, with a feeling of perfect peace and composure."

This voyage, boisterous as it was, proved beneficial, and was seconded by the bland airs of the Isle of France; so that the family at last returned to Maulmain, bearing with them only one invalid. Poor little "Pwen" was still a sufferer; and although he was considered convalescent, it was a long time before he fully recovered.

After these severe trials, Mrs. Judson returned to her accustomed labors, walking in the same toilsome, unostentatious path as before—writing, translating, teaching, advising, reproving, encouraging, and praying. Thus, years passed by, scarce noted, except upon the page of the Recording Angel. Some of the literary performances of this closing part of her life, are thus briefly mentioned in the Obituary Notice, by her husband:—"Her translation of the Pilgrim's Progress, Part 1st, into Burmese, is one of the best pieces of composition which we have yet published. Her translation of Mr. Boardman's 'Dying Father's Advice,' has become one of our standard tracts; and her hymns in Burmese, about twenty in number, are probably the best in our Chapel Hymn Book—a work which she was appointed by the Mission to edit. Beside these works, she published four volumes of Scripture Questions, which are in constant use in our Sabbath Schools." It has been remarked that the translation of the Pilgrim's Progress into an Eastern tongue, is "a work worth living for, if it were one's only performance." It was indeed a laborious work—under the circumstances, exceedingly laborious; and is performed as only one, who knew and loved the language as she did, assisted by her native genius, could perform it. She also contributed some valuable articles to the Burmese newspapers; and in the absence of Mr. Stevens, its able conductor, she was two or three times called upon to take the editorial charge of it. Her Sabbath Cards, with the breathings of her devotional and poetic spirit yet warm upon their surface, (her last, dying gift to the Burman church) are circulated from hand to hand; her Scripture questions furnish hundreds of bewildered minds with the clue to many a fountain, bubbling over with the fresh waters of truth and wisdom; and her sweet hymns are heard wherever the living God is worshipped, throughout this heathen land. The care of a very young and increasing family, where only the most inefficient service can be procured, would seem quite enough to occupy all of a mother's attention; but, how or when, none knew, she managed to find many a moment, which future time will multiply to years of usefulness. The inordinate desire for post-humous fame, which is made so poetical by those who wear out their lives in efforts to win it, is really scarce less contemptible, than any other utterly selfish passion—vanity, or even avarice. But it is a glorious thought to the Christian, that he may still guide the faltering footsteps of a brother, and add jewels to his Master's crown, when his voice is hushed in the grave, and his moldering hand lies as powerless as the dust with which it mingles. And doubly sweet must be the consolations of the dying-bed, when the glad prospect has not been purchased at the expense of lowlier daily duties. Such duties we have seen that Mrs. Judson never neglected, and even in life she reaped the sweet fruit of her toils.

> "None knew her but to love her,
> None named her but to praise,"

is perhaps the shortest mode of expressing the sentiments, that are heard in various forms, from many a lip; and this estimate is, by no means, confined to her own countrywomen. She avoided society, because it interfered with important pursuits, and not from any approach to asceticism; but she still had warm friends beyond the pleasant missionary circle. This appreciation and love, however, was not her sweetest reward. In April, 1844, she thus writes, "The state of religion is now very interesting in the Burman church. It would do your heart good to look in upon our little circle of praying Burman females. So humble, so devout, so willing to confess their faults before God and before one another, that I sometimes think Christians, in a Christian land, might well copy after them. I think they do strive to walk in the footsteps of our blessed Saviour. The study of the Scriptures and social prayer seem to be greatly blessed to their souls. Some of them have formed themselves into a Bible Class, and meet with me once a week, for the purpose of studying the Scriptures. They are now examining the 'Life of Christ,' with 'Questions,' which I prepared on the work some years ago. I think it does my own soul good, thus to ponder over the life of our blessed Lord. This Bible Class has increased, from about five to upwards of fifteen, within the last few months, and I see no signs of the number's diminishing. Some of them are quite elderly women, with gray hairs. You would be pleased to see them, with their spectacles on, sitting in a circle, reading the life of our Lord Jesus Christ, and conversing with each other, respecting their duty. One of them, upwards of seventy years old, amused me a few days ago, by saying she was the same age of my little daughter Abby-Ann. I asked her what she meant by that. She replied that she was converted the year that Abby-Ann was born, and it was not till then that she began to live."

In the last of her letters that I have in my possession, she says, "It is nineteen years, last month, since I parted with you, and bade adieu to my native land; and I can say, with unfeigned gratitude to God, that amid all the vicissitudes through which I have been called to pass, I have never, for one moment, regretted that I had entered the missionary field. We are not weary of our work—it is in our hearts to live and die among these people. I feel conscious of being a most unworthy, and unprofitable servant; and I often wonder that my life has been spared, while so many, to human view so much more competent than myself, have been cut down. 'Even so, Father, for so it seemeth good in Thy sight.'"

These nineteen years had, of necessity, wrought many changes; but they were like the changes which autumn perfects in the fruit-buds of spring. The eye was not so full of vivacity as formerly; and there was at times a pensive drooping of the lid, which spoke of familiarity with tears; but they were not tears to dim the centred light of a quiet, serene—I had almost said *holy*—happiness. The cheek had lost some of its roundness, and the skin its fairness; but the beauty of the ripening spirit had gradually stolen out upon the face, and none could regret the exchange. The step was not quite so elastic as in former days, but it had gained in freedom and stateliness; and though the figure exhibited none of the fragility, sometimes mistaken for grace of outline and proportion, there was more than enough to compensate, in the full, healthful development, seen much oftener in the women of England than those of America. The fresh-hearted maiden was transformed into the wife and mother;—the teacher of little bright-cheeked New England girls, was the guide of gray-haired heathen women, blinded by idolatry; but she was fresh-hearted still. Disappointment had passed over her, but it had left no blight; sorrow had wrung tears from her eyes, but they had fallen back upon her spirit, a fertilizing dew; trials had risen in her path, like flames, to scorch and wither, but she meekly bowed her heart to the Hand that sent them, and so they consumed only the alloy, and passed away, leaving the gold purified and burnished; and the death of beloved ones had only served to unlock a door between her soul and Heaven. Since the time of her first child's death, her course had been gradually upward. Her life had increased in holiness, and her spirit in meekness; for she had grown familiar with the one spot, where the unquiet human soul may find rest—deep in the shadow of the Cross. The first impulse of life, in the spirit of the young Christian, was, is the quick, joyous up-shooting of the green blade in spring. Next, her course through the world was shaped—the ear of corn was fashioned, and stood in the field, light, graceful, and fresh in summer verdure. But at length it began to bow beneath the weight of its own wealth, the green sheath gradually swelled with the increasing richness of its treasure; then the grain grew golden with ripeness; and angel reapers stood ready to dissever the drooping stem, and bear home the perfected fruit to the harvest of glory.

Chapter 15

THE CHRISTIAN'S DEATH

"Her suffering ended with the day,
Yet lived she at its close;
And breathed the long, long night away,
In statue-like repose.

But when the sun, in all his state,
Illumed the eastern skies,
She passed through Glory's morning-gate,
And walked in Paradise!"

—*Aldrich.*

After the birth of a child, in December, 1844—the flaxen-haired, sleek-shouldered boy, whose large, melting blue eyes follow the movements of my pen, in wondering-silence, as it traces these lines—Mrs. Judson visibly declined. She had been some months previous to this event suffering under the wasting disease, which had followed close upon her track, like the shadow of Death, since the first week, of her arrival in Burmah. But she had endured so much, and yet lived, had successfully resisted so many times, that it seemed scarce possible the place, which she had so long occupied in the dear heaven of earthly love, must be for ever darkened. The skill of the physician was taxed to its utmost; the kindness of the friend and the tenderness of the husband, each strove unweariedly, in turn and together—there were wet eyes, and bended knees, and prayerful voices, but the Mighty One bent not His ear: His own wisdom had marked for her a better way than their affection had power to devise.

A kind invitation from the Commissioner of Maulmain to accompany his family in an excursion down the coast, gave her, for several weeks, the benefit of sea-air; and though she speaks of her sufferings as sometimes indescribably severe, during this voyage, and returned, paler, thinner and weaker than she left, it was still hoped, that she had made some little improvement. But the hope soon faded; she declined from day to day—always a little thinner, and a little weaker, but cheerful still—till at last a voyage to America was named, as presenting the only prospect of life. To America! the land of her birth, and the home of many a loved one; where parents, brothers and sisters still trod the soil, and where her darling, her orphan boy might, once again, be folded to her bosom! Oh, should she visit dear, Christian America once more? Yet she could not leave those for whom she had toiled and prayed, during twenty years of exile, without sadness. Had it been right, she would have preferred to die quietly in Burmah, rather than interrupt her husband's labors; and her heart sunk at parting, for years, if not for life, with the most helpless of her babes—the eldest of the three, only four years of age. But duty demanded the sacrifice; and she had too long been obedient to this voice, to think of opposition now. They bore her to the ship, while both fair and dusky faces circled round; and long did the sound of those loved, farewell voices, half-smothered in grief and choked with tears, dwell upon her ear and heart. Near the Isle of France, hope of final recovery grew so strong, that it became almost certainty, (as much certainty as ever attends the prospects of mortals) and now a voice from poor, perishing Burmah seemed calling on the invalid for one more sacrifice. She dared not go back herself, but there seemed no longer a necessity for calling her husband from his missionary labor. He should return to his lonely home, and she, with her children, would pursue a way as lonely toward the "setting sun."

It was after this resolution that the following lines, the last words ever traced by her fingers, were penciled on a scrap of broken paper:

"We part on this green islet, Love,
Thou for the Eastern main,
I, for the setting sun, Love—
Oh, when to meet again?

My heart is sad for thee, Love,
For lone thy way will be;
And oft thy tears will fall, Love,
For thy children and for me.

The music of thy daughter's voice
Thou'lt miss for many a year;
And the merry shout of thine elder boys,
Thou'lt list in vain to hear.

When we knelt to see our Henry die,
And heard his last faint moan,
Each wiped away the other's tears—
Now, each must weep alone.

My tears fall fast for thee, Love,—
How can I say farewell?
But go;—thy God be with thee, Love,
Thy heart's deep grief to quell!

Yet my spirit clings to thine, Love,
Thy soul remains with me,
And oft we'll hold communion sweet,
O'er the dark and distant sea.

And who can paint our mutual joy,

When, all our wanderings o'er,
We both shall clasp our infants three,
At home, on Burmah's shore.

But higher shall our raptures glow,
On yon celestial plain,
When the loved and parted here below
Meet, ne'er to part again.

Then gird thine armor on, Love,
Nor faint thou by the way,
Till Boodh shall fall, and Burmah's sons
Shall own Messiah's sway."

"In all the missionary annals," says the editor of the New-York Evangelist, "there are few things more affecting than this. Mrs. Judson's beautiful lines remind us of Bishop Heber's verses addressed to his wife, 'If thou wert by my side, my love;' but they are superior in deep, natural feeling. How exquisite the references to her husband's anticipated loneliness! *'The music of thy daughter's voice, thou'lt miss for many a year!'* These verses make us think of the refinement, the exquisite sensibility, the tender affection, the deep and fervent piety of many a missionary wife among the heathen. Some of the most admirable women ever born have laid down their lives there, and some are still shedding the sweet light and grace of their holy, patient example, where few, besides the Saviour, can see and appreciate their labors. Oh, great will be their reward in heaven, when from every ingredient of bitterness and trial, in their earthly pilgrimage, there shall spring a harvest of eternal blessedness and glory. There will be no dearer, sweeter remembrances in heaven, than those of the painful earthly trials of their self-denying, desert-path for Christ. Dr. Judson is an old Christian soldier, but he never heard a more animating and sustaining word, amidst his conflicts, than the parting song of his wife. It will ring in his ear till he dies, and then again he will hear her angel-voice in heaven:—

'Then gird thine armor on, Love,
Nor faint thou by the way,
Till Boodh shall fall, and Burmah's sons
Shall own Messiah's sway!'"

But the anticipated sacrifice was not permitted. After their arrival at the island, she faded very perceptibly; and "withering—still withering," was once again borne back to the ship. And now we have the tender watching, the grateful smile, the bitter anguish of anticipated separation, and the soothing voice of love, winged for a flight to heaven; and above, and around, and closely blent with all—mingling, in dreams, in prayers, in hourly thoughts and spirit-crushing anticipations, the sweet, beautiful resignation, which none but the disciple of Christ can ever understand. Yet—must those blue waves indeed become the restless sepulchre of her precious dust? It was a sad thought; not to her who lay in her sweet smiles, waiting the withdrawal of her breath; but to him, the real sufferer, who leaned in uncomplaining agony over her pillow. Yet this, thank God! is spared. Behold yon rocky island! we make for port!

Whence the tears in those young eyes, as the small feet draw near, and the lips are bent to give the good-night kiss? and what means the low, mournful, but inimitably sweet murmur of voices, that swells and dies on the evening air? Oh, he that wept but at a brother's death, must look with peculiar tenderness on a scene like this!—childhood's last farewell breathed on a dying mother's lips.

It is morning, and all is over. The white "drapery of death lies quiet on the bosom cold;" and the wearied mourner sleeps peacefully, not far from the side of his beloved dead. And now, small feet are again astir, and rosy lips grow tremulous with sorrow. Turn we from those tears and sobs; for it is a mournful thing to look upon the grief of little hearts, for the first time wrung by the bitter anguish of the world, and with but the voice of a bereaved father to soothe them.

Colors are floating at half-mast in various directions; men bear about with them sad faces; and yonder, in the deep, heavy shadow of that overhanging-tree, they are breaking up the earth for the missionary's grave. Now, they lower the coffin over the vessel's side, and arrange the mourners. They are blunt men, but of a true and generous mold, that wear the weeds of sympathetic sorrow; for the heart of the bold seaman is throbbing in their bosoms; and they recollect a fading figure, that used sometimes to glide along the deck like a spirit, wearing ever a beautiful spirit-smile. Slowly and heavily beat the oars, and slowly, boat behind boat, moves the mournful procession to the shore. The waiting crowd falls back in silence; and tears involuntarily creep to stranger-eyes, as they look upon the little group about to leave the dearest of earthly treasures, and pursue their desolate journey, widowed and orphaned. Now, softly lift her to the bier, and give the heavy pall into gentle fingers! Let the sympathizing beholders gather in the coffin's track, and now—move on!

"Mournfully, tenderly,
Bear onward the dead,
Where the Warriour has lain,
Let the Christian be laid;
No place more befitting,
Oh, Rock of the sea!
Never such treasure
Was hidden in thee!

Mournfully, tenderly,
Solemn and slow—
Tears are bedewing
The path, as ye go;
Kindred and strangers
Are mourners today;—
Gently—so, gently—
Oh, bear her away.

Mournfully, tenderly,
Gaze on that brow;
Beautiful is it
In quietude now!
One look—and then settle
The loved to her rest,
The ocean beneath her,
The turf on her breast.

So have ye buried her—
Up!—and depart,
To life and to duty,
With undismayed heart!
Fear not; for the love
Of the stranger will keep
The casket that lies
In the Rock of the deep.

Peace, peace to thy bosom,
Thou servant of God!
The vale thou art treading
Thou hast before trod:
Precious dust thou hast laid
By the Hopia tree,
And treasure as precious
In the Rock of the sea."[1]

With the shaded grave at St. Helena, close I my tale; having reserved, for these last pages, some of the reminiscences, penned soon after his deep bereavement, by one who knew and loved the sleeper well.

After giving a brief sketch of her life, the Obituary thus

1 H. S. Washburn.

continues: "Her bereaved husband is the more desirous of bearing this testimony to her various attainments, her labors and her worth, from the fact that her own unobtrusive and retiring disposition always led her to seek the shade; as well as, from the fact that she was often brought into comparison with one whose life and character was uncommonly interesting and brilliant. The Memoir of his first beloved wife has been long before the public. It is, therefore, most gratifying to his feelings to be able to say in truth, that the subject of this notice was, in every point of natural and moral excellence, the worthy successor of Ann H. Judson. He constantly thanks God that he has been blest with two of the best of wives; he deeply feels that he has not improved those rich blessings as he ought; and it is most painful to reflect, that from the peculiar pressure of the missionary life, he has sometimes failed to treat those dear beings with that consideration, attention, and kindness, which their situation in a foreign heathen land ever demanded.

But to show the forgiving and grateful disposition of the subject of this sketch, and somewhat to elucidate her character, he would add that a few days before her death, he called her children to her bedside, and said, in their hearing, 'I wish, my love, to ask pardon for every unkind word or deed of which I have ever been guilty. I feel that I have, in many instances, failed of treating you with that kindness and affection which you have ever deserved.' 'Oh,' said she, 'you will kill me if you talk so. It is I that should ask pardon of you; and I only want to get well, that I may have an opportunity of making some return for all your kindness, and of showing you how much I love you.'

This recollection of her dying bed, leads me to say a few words relative to the closing scenes of her life. After her prostration at the Isle of France, where we spent three weeks, there remained but little expectation of her recovery. Her hope had long been fixed on the Rock of Ages, and she had been in the habit of contemplating death as neither distant nor undesirable. As it drew near, she remained perfectly tranquil. No shade of doubt, or fear, or anxiety, ever passed over her mind. She had a prevailing preference to depart and be with Christ. 'I am longing to depart,' and 'what can I want besides?' quoting the language of a familiar hymn, were the expressions which revealed the spiritual peace and joy of her mind; yet, at times, the thought of her native land, to which she was approaching after an absence of twenty years, and a longing desire to see once more her son George, her parents, and the friends of her youth, drew down her ascending soul, and constrained her to say, 'I am in a strait betwixt two—let the will of God be done.'

In regard to her children she ever manifested the most surprising composure and resignation, so much so, that I was once induced to say 'You seem to have forgotten the dear little ones we have left behind.' 'Can a mother forget'—she replied, and was unable to proceed. During her last days, she spent much of her time in praying for the early conversion of her children. May her living and her dying prayers draw down the blessing of God on their bereaved heads.

On our passage homeward, as the strength of Mrs. J. gradually declined, I expected to be under the painful necessity of burying her in the sea. But it was so ordered in Divine Providence, that when the indications of approaching death had become strongly marked, the ship came to anchor in the port of St. Helena. For three days she continued to sink rapidly, though her bodily sufferings were not very severe. Her mind became liable to wander, but a single word was sufficient to recall and steady her recollections. On the evening of the 31st of August, she appeared to be drawing near to the end of her pilgrimage: The children took leave of her and retired to rest. I sat alone by the side of her bed during the hours of the night, endeavoring to administer relief to the distressed body and consolation to the departing soul. At two o'clock in the morning, wishing to obtain one more token of recognition, I roused her attention, and said, 'Do you still love the Saviour?' 'Oh yes,' she replied, 'I ever love the Lord Jesus Christ.' I said again, 'Do you still love me?' She replied in the affirmative, by a peculiar expression of her own.

'Then give me one more kiss;' and we exchanged that token of love for the last time. Another hour passed—life continued to recede—and she ceased to breathe. For a moment I traced her upward flight, and thought of the wonders which were opening to her view. I then closed her sightless eyes, dressed her, for the last time, in the drapery of death; and being quite exhausted with many sleepless nights, I threw myself down and slept. On awaking in the morning, I saw the children standing and weeping around the body of their dear mother, then, for the first time, inattentive to their cries. In the course of the day, a coffin was procured from the shore, in which I placed all that remained of her whom I had so much loved; and after a prayer had been offered by a dear brother minister from the town, the Rev. Mr. Bertram, we proceeded in boats to the shore. There we were met by the Colonial chaplain, and accompanied to the burial-ground by the adherents and friends of Mr. Bertram, and a large concourse of the inhabitants. They had prepared the grave in a beautiful, shady spot, contiguous to the grave of Mrs. Chater, a missionary from Ceylon, who had died in similar circumstances on her passage home. There I saw her safely deposited; and in the language of prayer, which we had often presented together at the throne of grace, I blessed God that her body had attained the repose of the grave, and her spirit the repose of Paradise. After the funeral, the dear friends of Mr. Bertram took me to their houses and their hearts; and their conversation and prayers afforded me unexpected relief and consolation. But I was obliged to hasten on board ship, and we immediately went to sea. On the following morning no vestige of the island was discernible in the distant horizon. For a few days, in the solitude of my cabin, with my poor children crying around me, I could not help abandoning myself to heart-breaking sorrow. But the promises of the gospel came to my aid, and faith stretched her view to the bright world of eternal life, and anticipated a happy meeting with those beloved beings, whose bodies are moldering at Amherst and St. Helena.

I exceedingly regret that there is no portrait of the second, as of the first Mrs. Judson. Her soft blue eye, her mild aspect, her lovely face and elegant form, have never been delineated on canvass. They must soon pass away from the memory, even of her children; but they will remain for ever enshrined in her husband's heart.

To my friends at St. Helena, I am under great obligations. Receiving the body of the deceased from my hands as a sacred deposit, they united with our kind captain, in defraying all the expenses of the funeral, and promised to take care of the grave, and superintend the erection of the grave-stones, which I am to forward; and on which I propose to place the following inscription:—

Sacred to the Memory of Sarah B. Judson, member of the American Baptist Mission to Burmah; formerly wife of the Rev. George D. Boardman, of Tavoy, and lately, wife of the Rev. Adoniram Judson, of Maulmain—who died in this port Sept. 1, 1845, on her passage to the United States, in the 42nd year of her age, and the 21st of her missionary life.

She sleeps sweetly here on this rock of the ocean,
Away from the home of her youth,
And far from the land where with heartfelt devotion,
She scattered the bright beams of truth."

A. J.

Boston, Oct. 1845.

A TRIBUTE

OFF ST. HELENA, SEPT. 1846.

Blow softly, gales! a tender sigh
Is flung upon your wing;
Lose not the treasure, as ye fly,
Bear it where love and beauty lie,
Silent and withering.

Flow gently, waves! a tear is laid
Upon your heaving breast;

Leave it within yon dark rock's shade,
Or weave it in an iris braid,
To crown the Christian's rest.

Bloom, ocean-isle! lone ocean-isle!
Thou keep'st a jewel rare;
Let rugged rock and dark defile,
Above the slumbering stranger smile,
And deck her couch with care.

Weep, ye bereaved! a dearer head
Ne'er left the pillowing breast;
The good, the pure, the lovely fled,
When, mingling with the shadowy dead,
She meekly went to rest.

Mourn, Burmah, mourn! a bow which spanned
Thy cloud, has passed away;
A flower has withered on thy sand,
A pitying spirit left thy strand;
A saint has ceased to pray.

Angels, rejoice! another string
Has caught the strains above;
Rejoice, rejoice! a new-fledged wing
Around the Throne is hovering,
In sweet, glad, wondering love.

Blow, blow, ye gales! wild billows roll!
Unfurl the canvass wide!
On! where she labored lies our goal;—
Weak, timid, frail, yet would my soul
Fain be to hers allied.

NOTES TO THE MEMOIR OF SARAH B. JUDSON

NOTE 1
PREVALENCE OF BOODHISM.

"Pity the deluded nations,
Wrapped in shades of dismal night."—page 24.

It will be observed, that among the several religions which the writer of this poem has mentioned, that of the people to whose improvement she afterward devoted herself, is omitted. Boodhism was for many years confounded with Brahminism: and though it is now ascertained to be a distinct system, spreading itself over some of the most populous portions of the globe, it is still comparatively unknown.

Boodhism took its rise, about 600 years before Christ, in Central India, where the antiquarian still finds ample proof of its former prevalence. It was banished from India by the Brahmins; but still prevails in Ceylon; and has spread itself over Burmah, Siam, Cochinia, China, Tartary, and Japan. It is also, in a modified form, the religion of Thibet—the Grand Lama being a sort of demi-Boodh. In China, it is somewhat corrupted by Shamanism; and in Burmah, especially among the Peguan part of the population, by Nat worship, from both of which Boodhism, in its original purity, is quite distinct. The system of Confucius also prevails, to some extent, in China; but the popular religion is the same as in the neighboring nations—*Foe* or *Fuh* being the Chinese pronunciation of the Pali *Boodha*.

When the populousness of the regions, where this system of religion flourishes, is considered, some conception may be formed of its great prevalence; and, by taking the usual estimate of other religions for data, we may arrive at still more definite conclusions. The four prevailing systems of religion, now in the world, are Christianity, in its different forms, Mahometanism, Brahminism, and Boodhism. These comprise about nine-tenths of the One Thousand Millions, at which the population of the earth is estimated; the residue, exclusive of ten millions of Jews, being made up of wild nomadic tribes, and isolated islanders, with various local superstitions, but with no settled form of religion. Protestant Christians are estimated at sixty-five millions; Nominal Christians—Romanists, Greeks, and Armenians, collectively, at one hundred and eighty-five millions; Mahometans, at one hundred and forty millions; Brahminists, nearly one hundred millions; and Boodhists, probably, number above four hundred millions—or as many as the other false systems, and the corrupted forms of Christianity combined.

NOTE 2
KYOUNGS AND PRIESTS.

"And still beneath the carved gables, and glittering spires of the Kyoung, swarmed yellow-robed, indolent priests."—page 26.

A KYOUNG IS A BURMESE MONASTERY. Though sometimes quite plain in its style of building, it is usually profusely ornamented with minute and curious carvings, and surmounted by a graduated roof, which presents numerous gables on every side, and bristles with small gilded spires. The rank of the occupant is ascertained by the number of gradations in the roof. The Burmese, when about to erect a kyoung, choose the finest site—a rising spot of ground, sufficiently spacious to convert the noise of the busy world without, into a distant, pleasing hum. The clear waters of an artificial pool sparkle in the vicinity; images of gilded wood or of alabaster are elevated on small thrones, lodged in the branches of the sacred banian, and enclosed in shrines, which are scattered, here and there, among its fruit-trees; a few richly-scented flowers are allowed to bud and blossom in the cool shadows; and the whole scene is overlooked by a neighboring pagoda, whose little gilded bells, kept in motion by the air, create a continual, low, murmuring music. The numerous small pagodas, which cluster around the large one, are interspersed with temples and shrines of various descriptions; and, here and there, towers a tall flag-staff, with a group of fabulous monsters near the top, and beneath them, a long, gauze cylinder, glittering with tinsel, streaming out upon the air. When a Burman draws near one of these quiet and beautiful places, he reverently bares his feet, for to him it is holy ground.

The priests of Boodh practice the strictest celibacy; and thus their system differs essentially from that of the Brahmins, whose priesthood is hereditary. Brahminical priests, by observing the sanctity of their caste, and keeping aloof from other men, are regarded as a superior order of beings; but though this practice is calculated to inspire the greater awe, the Boodhistic priesthood, from having its roots in almost every family of respectability throughout the empire, has a far stronger hold on the affections of the people. The priests, in Burmah, are supported by voluntary contributions. It is customary for them to go out every morning, each bearing his own rice-pot, which, as they pass from house to house, never looking in at the door, except as they are invited, grows heavy with the liberality of their worshippers. On great festival days, each district prepares an artificial tree, which, being laden with gifts, is carried at the head of a long, gaily-dressed train of persons, each bearing a well-filled vessel, lavishly ornamented with flowers and tinsel. The priests are also the schoolmasters of the nation; and the gifts, which they receive from their numerous pupils, contribute essentially to their support. Every rainy season, the boys flock to the kyoungs for instruction; and nearly every man of respectability in the empire, has worn the yellow cloth, through a novitiatory term of two or three seasons. Thus the religion of the Burman enters deeply into all his early and more pleasing associations; and, in process of time, becomes entwined with the very fibres of his nationality; so that he literally *forsakes all*, when he embraces Christianity.

NOTE 3
ANN H. JUDSON.

"True greatness, after it has once been developed, bears always with it a consciousness of power, perfectly consistent with feminine delicacy, and Christian humility."—page 38.

It is sometimes thought, that the higher attributes of intellect are incompatible with those gentle and winning virtues, essential to the completeness of female character. Whether this opinion be in general correct or otherwise, the life of Ann H. Judson affords a beautiful example of the union of Christian heroism with the most attractive feminine excellence. She is known to the world, through her brilliant and striking traits of character; but there are a few hearts in which her softer and more retiring virtues have reared a no less enviable mausoleum. Two ladies, who knew her somewhat intimately, were once describing her as a person of "queenly" presence; when one of them, (Mrs. Wade,) added, "But it was not for that, nor for her superior intellect, that I loved her so dearly. With all her dignity, she was simple, affable and affectionate; and young and inexperienced as I was, she treated me, during the long passage out, and ever after, not only with the kind consideration of an endeared friend, but with the sympathizing tenderness of a sister."

I need offer no apology for presenting one of the many anecdotes, which serve to exhibit her character in its strictly feminine developments. During the early part of her residence in Rangoon, she discovered by the river side a poor family, with a sick and suffering little child. Of the parents, who were Anglo-Indians, she knew nothing, except that they were strangers in a foreign port, and in distress; but it needed no more to enlist her ever-active sympathies in their behalf. The house was at the distance of a mile from the Mission premises: yet she walked to and fro daily, and watched over her little charge with the patient, tender solicitude of a mother. But, with all her care, the poor child died. She dressed it in its little shroud, accompanied it to the grave, and returned to her home, followed by the blessings of the bereaved and inconsolable parents. Close by the house of the poor East-Indian, two English ship-captains had a temporary residence, and they watched her movements in wondering admiration; one of them, as was afterward reported, frequently exclaiming, "That is strange!—that is wonderful!—that must be true religion!" Shortly after this, Mrs. Judson became ill; and it was thought necessary for her to proceed to Madras for medical advice. The person to whom application was made for a passage, proved to be one of the neighbors of the bereaved Indian. He waited only to hear the name of his proposed passenger, when he burst forth in an enthusiastic panegyric, concluding with, "Most gladly will I take her, but without any charges; my vessel is only too much honored by carrying freight like that."

Her character as a mother was never fully developed; for her children died in infancy; but as a wife, few have had opportunity to exhibit such unwavering devotion, through scenes of indescribable peril and suffering. But even here, one phase only of her character is visible; and, with such evidences of heroism before our eyes, we can scarcely think of her as the gentle, confiding wife, that she really was. In looking over some old papers, I have found a touchingly tender letter, addressed to her husband, during his first considerable absence, in which occur the following lines, evidently an impromptu:

"As the frail ivy twines around
The firm and stately tree,
So you, my love, too late I've found
Have been the elm to me.

As shines the moon, serene and high,
In borrowed light arrayed,
So you the sun have been, while I
Have but your light displayed."

NOTE 4
THE ENGLISH AND BURMESE WAR.

"But an unexpected voice came up from Bengal—the roar of cannon, and the clash of arms."—page 40.

The Burmans had, for many years, made themselves annoying, if not dangerous, to their European neighbors, by such a series of unprovoked, petty aggressions, as only a proud, semi-civilized people would be guilty of perpetrating. Emboldened by the forbearance of the "white foreigners," which they ascribed to timidity, they grew more impudent in their aggressions; and finally proceeded to surprise a small outpost, and to massacre two companies of seapoys, with their European officers. Elated with their temporary success, they next conceived the plan of "driving the English from India." With this object in view, an army was ordered to proceed over land to Calcutta, taking in its route an indefinite number of towns, concerning the locality of which, its leaders were profoundly ignorant. Mr. and Mrs. Judson, in their journey from Rangoon to Ava, met this army proceeding down the Irrawaddy, under the command of the Burmese general, Ban-doo-lah. Before the Burmans had completed their tardy preparations for the contemplated invasion, they were suddenly surprised by an English fleet off Rangoon, and obliged to turn their attention to the defense of their own territory.

The unexpected and formidable enemy, after possessing themselves of this port, moved slowly up the river, making pacific overtures at every considerable advance. But though their movements would have been truly alarming to people better instructed in the art of war, the ignorant and haughty Burmans treated every conciliatory intimation with disdain. On moved the all-conquering English, in spite of wooden stockades, burning rafts, and other defensive preparations, until within forty miles of Ava. The Burmese army had been defeated at every turn; and now the report that the presumptuous foreigners actually meditated an attack upon the golden city, spread universal consternation. But it was not until the threat of the "Cock-feather General," (Sir Archibald Campbell—so called from his military plume) to blow up the palace, if he once gained sight of its spire, had reached the royal ears, that commissioners from the king were despatched to meet him, with instructions to make a treaty of peace.

NOTE 5
THE TREATY, AND ITS RESULTS TO THE MISSION.

"It now became the first business of the Missionaries to find some spot under the British Government," etc.—page 42.

In consequence of various disastrous circumstances, which a more definite knowledge of the country might probably have averted, the expedition against the Burmans was rendered very expensive to the English Government. By the treaty of Yan-da-bo, the Court of Ava became pledged to pay One Crore of Rupees, (about Five Millions of Dollars)—a small part only of the actual expenses of the war; and also ceded to the conquerors the Provinces of Arracan and Tenasserim. The latter is a strip of territory, from forty to eighty miles wide, stretching along the coast about five hundred miles, and including the Provinces of Amherst (or Maulmain) Tavoy, and Mergui. The first attempt to erect an English town was made in Amherst Province, at the mouth of the Martaban River; but the plan was subsequently abandoned, and Maulmain, twenty miles farther north, eventually became the seat of trade and government.

The immediate effects of the war on the infant mission were disastrous in the extreme; for the Burmans naturally confounded Americans, whose dress, language and habits so closely resembled those of the English, with their enemies; and consequently, the missionaries became objects of suspicion and dread. The treaty provided for a British Resident at the court; but though he might protect their persons from violence, he had no power to secure toleration to their religion, which had now become more distasteful than ever, to the humbled officers of government. Accordingly, most of the missionaries repaired to the Provinces, where they established permanent stations. While the British Resident remained at the court, efforts were made, from time to time, by different missionaries, to maintain a footing in the empire; but on his expulsion in 1838, they deemed it prudent to withdraw; and since that time no successful attempt has been made to carry the Christian religion to the capital. The Burmese law, prohibiting the emigration of females, and the practice of visiting its infringement with unrelenting severity, upon the nearest remaining relatives, prevented, to a great extent, the increase of population in the Tenasserim Provinces; but, by a census taken in 1839, the Burmese and Peguans, (the latter by far the more numerous) are ascertained to number 92,242. This presents no very contracted field of labor, except when placed in comparison with the millions of Burmah, who, by the intolerance of their rulers, are, for the present, deprived of the means of salvation. Without attempting to fathom the councils of the Almighty, we may cheerfully confide in the wisdom of his plans, feeling assured that he knows precisely the strength of his enemies, and the weapons necessary for their overthrow. His ultimate designs in regard to the time and means of renovating Burmah, futurity must disclose; but thus far, he has so ordered events, that while the work of personal conversion has not progressed rapidly, a broad and firm basis has been laid for the final superstructure. No pressing call for books has led to the consumption of time and money in imperfect, ephemeral productions; but most of the literary productions of the missionaries have been the result of severe study, and are of such a character as will insure for them ultimate permanency, as standard works. The language has been adapted with such laborious nicety to the Christian religion, and to Western science, and the idiom so accurately preserved, that an intelligent Burman has little difficulty in understanding propositions entirely novel, frequently finding in nomenclature merely, neat explanations of abstruse points. It is not to be supposed, however, that the edicts of a heathen monarch, have been permitted to shut the gospel wholly from the empire. Beside the seed scattered in former years, and left to germinate under the influences of the Spirit, many a visitor, hearing in Maulmain of the eternal God, goes back to whisper the wonderful truth on the banks of the Irrawaddy; and many a petty trader, seeking worldly gain only, bears to his far home, in the shape of a prohibited book, hidden in some secret corner of his boat, imperishable treasure.

NOTE 6
BAMBOO HOUSES.

"A small bamboo house, a very frail shelter in the eyes of an American, was erected for them at Maulmain."—page 48.

THESE SIMPLE ABODES OF THE early missionaries were sufficiently unique to deserve a passing notice. Excepting the roofs, which were thatched with a species of palm-leaf, or a coarse kind of wild grass, the whole of the materials were of bamboo—a plentiful, not altogether inelegant, though exceedingly fragile substitute for solid wood. As soon as a few boards could be obtained they were used to give greater firmness to the structure; but for a long time, nothing but the bamboo, split and woven into mats, formed the outer walls and partitions; and every timber, from pillar and cross-beam to rafter and lintel, was obtained from the same elephant species of the grass family. The floor was also woven, in the same fashion as the walls, admitting crevices so broad as to render much housewifely care unnecessary; bamboo chairs, couches, tables, etc., mostly fixtures, were arranged in convenient places; and the whole structure was elevated on hollow bamboo poles, above the miasma of the jungle, and beyond the reach of prowling wild beasts. The floors yielded to the tread, with an elasticity which detracted essentially from the pleasures of indoor exercise; but the foot, after a time, became so accustomed to the motion, that the sensation of stepping on boards is described as something like a sailor's impressions on touching *terra firma*. These dwellings, when new, have an agreeable air of freshness and cleanliness about them; but one who is desirous of giving a pleasing impression, will say nothing of them in their decay. The majority of native houses are still constructed mostly of bamboo.

NOTE 7
ZAYATS.

"My dear husband has just been repairing an old Zayat."—page 55.

A Zayat is an open shed, used for some public purpose. Zayats are usually erected by the way-side, at convenient distances, for affording a temporary shelter to travellers; and therefore they present favorable positions from which to dispense religious instruction. There are always several zayats in the neighborhood of a kyoung, to which the devotees of Boodh resort to listen to their priests; and, in general, like the markets of old, they are suitable and popular places for the discussion of all matters of public interest. The zayats owned by the Mission are occupied all day, either by a missionary or native assistant, who converses with those who will listen, and distributes books to those who will receive them; and though it has been found a wearisome duty, it has been productive of lasting results.

NOTE 8
THE KARENS.

"In February, 1829, Mr. Boardman made his first tour among the Karens."—page 56.

THE KARENS HAVE, FOR MANY years, been known to American Christians, and have shared deeply in their sympathies. Different opinions respecting their origin have, from time to time, been advanced; but who they are, or whence they came, if not indigenous to the Burmese wilderness, is still a mystery, even to themselves. Distant resemblances have been traced between the Karens and several mountain tribes to the north of Burmah; but nothing satisfactory with regard to their identity has yet been ascertained, and the whole subject is one of loose conjecture. Their numbers have also been variously estimated. By a census of the Tenasserim Provinces, taken in 1839, the Karens and Toung-thoos, (the latter a small hill tribe, not easily distinguished by a casual observer) were ascertained to number 13,503. This estimate includes those of both races, from the Province of Maulmain on the north, to Tavoy, and thence to Mergui on the south; but since that time, the number of Karens has been considerably increased by immigration, especially in the vicinity of Maulmain. They are probably four or five times as numerous in the southern part of Burmah, where they occupy a strip of territory lying between Rangoon and Bassein, and extending along the borders of Arracan; while a third division, still more numerous, people a range of hills stretching off to the north-east, as far as Toung-oo, an inland city, half-way between Rangoon and Ava. They are a rude, wandering race, drawing their principal support from the streams that flow through their valleys, and from the natural products of their native mountains. They migrate in small parties, and when they have found a favorable spot, fire the underbrush, and erect a cluster of three or four huts on the ashes. In the intervals of procuring food, the men have frequent occasion to hew out a canoe, or weave a basket; and the women manufacture a kind of cotton cloth, which furnishes material for the clothing of the family. Here they remain until they have exhausted the resources of the surrounding forest, when they seek out another spot, and repeat the same process.

The Karens are a meek, peaceful race, simple and credulous, with many of the softer virtues, and few flagrant vices. Though greatly addicted to drunkenness, extremely filthy, and indolent in their habits, their morals, in other respects, are superior to many more civilized races. Their traditions, like those of several tribes of American Indians, are a curious medley of truth and absurdity; but they have some tolerably definite ideas of a Great Being, who governs the universe; and many of their traditionary precepts bear a striking resemblance to those of the Gospel. They have various petty superstitions; but with the exception of a small division, known to the Burmans as Talaing Karens, and to the missionaries as Pghos or Shos, they have never adopted Boodhism—the oppressive treatment which they have received at the hands of their Burmese rulers, probably contributing to increase their aversion to idolatry.

Soon after the arrival of the first Burmese missionary in Rangoon, his attention was attracted by small parties of strange, wild-looking men, clad in unshapely garments, who, from time to time, straggled past his residence. He was told that they were called Karens; that they were more numerous than any similar tribe in the vicinity; and as untameable as the wild cow of the mountains. He was farther told, that they shrunk from association with other men, seldom entering a town, except on compulsion; and that, therefore, any attempt to bring them within the sphere of his influence would prove unsuccessful. His earnest inquiries, however, awakened an interest in the minds of the Burmese converts; and one of them finding, during the war, a poor Karen bond-servant in Rangoon, paid his debt, and thus became, according to the custom of the country, his temporary master. When peace was restored he was brought to the missionaries on the Tenasserim coast, and instructed in the principles of the

Christian religion. He eventually became the subject of regenerating grace, and proved a faithful and efficient evangelist. Through this man, who will be recognized as Ko-Thah-byoo, access was gained to others of his countrymen, and they listened with ready interest. They were naturally docile; they had no long-cherished prejudices, and time-honored customs to fetter them; and their traditions taught them to look for the arrival of white-faced foreigners from the West, who would make them acquainted with the true God. The missionaries, in their first communications with the Karens, were obliged to employ a Burmese interpreter; and notwithstanding the disadvantages under which they labored, the truth spread with great rapidity. Soon, however, Messrs. Wade and Mason devoted themselves to the acquisition of the language; and the former conferred an inestimable blessing on the race, by reducing it to writing. This gave a fresh impetus to the spread of Christianity. The wild men and women, in their mountain homes, found a new employment; and they entered upon it with enthusiastic avidity. They had never before supposed their language capable of being represented by signs, like other languages; and they felt themselves, from being a tribe of crushed, down-trodden slaves, suddenly elevated into a nation, with every facility for possessing a national literature. This had a tendency to check their roving propensities; and, under the protection of the British Government, they began to cultivate a few simple arts; though the most civilized among them still refuse to congregate in towns, and it is unusual to find a village that numbers more than five or six houses. Their first reading-books consisted of detached portions of the Gospel; and the Holy Spirit gave to the truth, thus communicated, regenerating power. Churches sprang up, dotting the wilderness like so many lighted tapers; and far back among the rocky fastnesses of the mountains, where foreign foot has never trod, the light is already kindled, and will continue to increase in brilliancy, till one of the darkest corners of the earth shall be completely illuminated.

NOTE 9
THE TAVOY REBELLION.

Chapter 8.

The more minute particulars of this chapter were obtained from a son of the friendly Mussulman, alluded to in the history, and from a Burmese convert, who was, at the time of the event, a pupil in Mr. Boardman's school. Mrs. Boardman left no record of her personal sufferings, during this week of terrors; and it has, therefore, been necessary to introduce a general outline of common dangers and sufferings, in which she bore a heavy share. The various by-tragedies, that were, from time to time, acted, as well as many items of more general interest, which could not be spared from a paper purporting to be a full history of the event, are, for obvious reasons, omitted. It may not, however, be improper to remark, in justice both to the native inhabitants of Tavoy, and their foreign rulers, that this rebellion originated, neither in oppressive treatment, on the one side, nor disaffection on the other. The leader of the revolt being of royal extraction, intended the restoration of the Tavoy Province, (with himself, of course, for viceroy) to the crown; a scheme which was sanctioned and assisted, if not concocted, by the powers at Ava. By means of flattering promises, he gained some restless and ambitious spirits to his cause; but the great body of the people participated in the revolt, only so far as was necessary to insure personal safety, and afterward returned to their allegiance without question or suspicion.

NOTE 10
HEATHEN WOMEN.

"His widow, who is not yet fifteen, is one of the loveliest of our desert blossoms."—page 101.

The spread of Christianity, within the last half century, has caused many such woodland blossoms to expand beneath the rays of the Sun of Righteousness. But though Mrs. Boardman was gifted with a genial heart, and a truly poetic eye, she discerned no loveliness in these degraded women of the wilderness, aside from the ornaments gathered from the Cross of Christ. Indeed, she was always the first to condemn the absurd fascinations, in which modern sentiment has seen fit to enshrine the "unsophisticated children of nature;" for though it is no agreeable task to mar a beautiful picture, poetry is degraded, by lending its graces to adorn that which is inherently vile. Oh, how would a refined nature shrink from actual association with the debased original of the artist's pencil and the poet's pen—the "wild child of freedom, all impulse and grace," as she really appears, divested of foreign ornament, in her native haunts! She is indeed "wild" and "free"—her wildness, untouched by the slightest refining influence, from within or without, and her freedom, that of the profligate son, among his swine and husks. She is a creature of "impulse"—such impulse as springs from the innate depravity of a thoroughly debased nature, which "from the sole of the foot even unto the head, has no soundness in it." During a few years of her life she may have animal beauty, and a degree of animal "grace;" but her face mirrors a vacant mind, save as it is occupied by the grossest cares, and her gracefulness emanates from no higher source than mere elasticity of muscle. She is thoroughly degraded, full of vile passions and base propensities, by which she renders herself despised; and even the very qualities which were originally intended to beautify the female character, and which makes woman honored and beloved in Christian lands, are so distorted, that their aim is lost, and they only serve to increase the general blackness and deformity. This is no over-wrought picture. Indeed the subject is of a nature which will not admit of the vividness of coloring necessary to present it in its true light. Oh, it sickens the very soul to look upon the vice and misery, into whose fearful depths all nations of the earth, unblest by gospel light, are plunged; but they who have no courage to look, cannot have the priceless privilege of alleviating. It is better, however, to shut the eyes forever, than to conjure up a brilliant fantasy, and lack the candor or discrimination to discern its fatal falseness. Let the highly favored daughter of America step from her refined Christian circle, into one of these heathen scenes—let but a single female heart be unveiled for her inspection, and how would she shudder, while she exclaimed, in disgust and shame: "Can this, indeed, be my sister? and is this but an exhibition of my own nature, in its uncleansed nakedness?" The general degradation of our race in heathen lands is increasingly appreciated, having engaged some of the most energetic efforts of the Church; but the degradation of women has never yet specifically asserted its peculiar and inalienable claim on woman's pity and benevolence.

NOTE 11
THE CREMATION OF PRIESTS.

"The whole town, male and female, from the infant to the grey-headed, are engaged in the ceremonies attendant on the burning of a priest, who died several months ago."—page 103.

THE CREMATION OF A PRIEST is conducted with great pomp and ceremony, and is one of the most showy and expensive, as well as the most exhilarating of Boodhistic festivities. This honor is paid to priests of high rank only, and is usually shared by several persons in concert; the bodies having been preserved for the occasion, by a process which reduces them to fleshless, cork-like mummies. The principal preparations for the festival are superintended by the head-men of the several districts; each district training its separate band of dancers and musicians, and contributing the usual glittering paraphernalia. The construction of an engine, which shall rival that of a neighboring district, in lighting the funeral pile, is the most important and difficult part of the preparation. A log of wood, bored and filled with gunpowder, constitutes the body of the machine, which is so planned as to act on nearly the same principle as a rocket; but as it is intended to run on the ground, instead of rising through the air, it is placed on wheels, and has, altogether, the appearance of a low car. The full-sized figure of a warrior, a white elephant, some fabulous monster, or whatever else fancy may design, standing in an imposing attitude, occupies the platform above the tube, and gives to the machine an appearance of animated life.

On the morning of the gala day, the various parties, decked in the gayest of their festive finery, and preceded by musicians and dancers, move in procession to the ground chosen for the exhibition—a large, open plain. The bodies of the dead (or rather *returned)* priests having been previously restored to their original comeliness, by a thick coating of wax, covered with gold leaf, are conveyed in the manner described by Mrs. Boardman. Companies of professional mourners follow the cars, and fill the air with their lamentations; and the bearers frequently pause, and turn their faces homeward, as though their grief was too great to allow them to proceed. When they reach the ground, the frail, but magnificent coffins, still surrounded by their gorgeous and combustible trappings, are placed on an elevated platform, having the faggots underneath, and canopied by a graduated roof, surmounted by a glittering spire. The musicians strike up some popular, sacred air, the dancers ply their art, and the competition commences. The rumbling of wheels, and the rushing sound of the firing engine, soon mingle with the shouts of the spectators; bets run high; and the interest becomes intense. Every eye in the vast multitude is fixed on the seemingly intelligent machine, as it hurries along the ground, leaving behind it a long train of fire and smoke, and each moment increasing its speed, as it draws near the combustible pyre. This amusement continues during the greater part of the day; the excitement of the throng deepening, as the contest advances to a close. At last the pile is lighted, and consumed with various ceremonies. The relics of the honored dead are usually collected and preserved in an urn; the crowds disperse; and the victorious party returns at nightfall, amid shouts of congratulation and triumphant rejoicings.

NOTE 12
CHARACTERISTICS OF BOODHISM.

"The Burman system of morality is superior to that of the nations around them, . . . and is surpassed only by the divine precepts of our blessed Saviour."—page 105.

Boodhism, like Brahminism, is founded on the Pythagorean doctrine of Metempsychosis, though it rejects the idea that One Living Principle pervades all nature. It teaches that the number of beings is infinite, and that the spiritual essence of each has been transmigrating through various conditions and modes of existence, from eternity; for the life of the spirit is without beginning. The state of the soul, during each stage of existence, and the manner of its development in animal form, are determined by its course through previous stages. The sentence, however, is not awarded by an intelligent arbiter, such a being having no place in the Boodhistic system. The sequence of events is determined by destiny; and as all moral acts are intrinsically good or evil, they are inevitably followed by the adequate reward or punishment, as effect follows cause, or "as the cart-wheel moves in the track of the ox." Since evil deeds cannot be pardoned or atoned for, there is no room for expiatory sacrifices; and therefore, the bloody rites of Brahminism are peculiarly abhorrent to Boodhists—their religion teaching that the destruction of animal life involves an incalculable amount of guilt, and, consequently, suffering.

Merit is obtained by obedience to the precepts of virtue, by the performance of benevolent deeds, and especially by making offerings to the priests; and at death, the soul ascends or descends in the scale of existence, as its merit or demerit preponderates. Thus all beings are continually revolving on the great "wheel of transmigration," from man to monster, or to the vilest reptile—from the celestial inhabitant of an upper heaven to the blackest demon in hell, with no hope of rest or reprieve, save in total extinction. And even this hope, desperate as it seems to the Christian, is one to which the mass of Boodhists scarcely venture to aspire. For, notwithstanding the number of divinities called Boodhs, that have passed into annihilation from eternity, are "as the sands on the banks of the Ganges," and each one has taken multitudes into this state with him, yet as the number of beings is infinite, the chance of becoming one of this favored class is to any individual incalculably small.

As a code of morals, the Boodhistic religion is unrivalled by any other merely human institution. The great leading commands of Gaudama are five, viz.:

Kill not.
Steal not.
Commit not adultery.
Speak not falsehood.
Drink not intoxicating liquor.

These, however, present but a bare outline of the system, as meagre as is the view given of the Christian faith by the ten Mosaic commandments. It is replete with high moral precepts, some of which are found among the leading principles of the Gospel. Kindness to an enemy, and the duty of returning good for evil, are inculcated among its most prominent doctrines; and in illustration of these principles, it is declared, that one of the highest acts of virtue man can perform, is "to give eyes, heart, and liver, to feed a hungry tiger." But there is one feature which mars the beauty of the entire picture. The wise framers of these laws were unaware of any higher motive than self-love, and so *self* is made the centre and circumference of the whole system. The principle of true benevolence is not recognized; and thus, even the superficial kind feeling, which puts on its semblance in all Christian communities, gives place to the most assured and undisguised selfishness. A man performs good actions with the sole view of benefiting himself; and when he receives good at the hands of another he is insusceptible of gratitude, for he understands the motive of his benefactor. If he takes any interest in the matter, he is ready to consider the favor reciprocal, or, perhaps, he envies the merit, to the attainment of which he has been made the stepping-stone. This one prominent feature of Boodhism, which places the system in a position antipodal to the Gospel, is at once its strength and its weakness. By accommodating itself to human frailty, it lays its foundations broad and firm; while, on the other hand, it so identifies itself with a perverted nature, as to be unable to beget true virtue, or to exist in a purer atmosphere. Thus, though this wide-spread scheme of religion has taxed the skill of the mere moralist to the utmost, it stands a monument of human inefficiency, as well as human ingenuity. It is like some cold, silent creation of the chisel, which displays the genius of the artist only—like its own soulless deities, a counterfeit presentment of life, which is yet forever dead. It commends itself to the intellect, but cannot reach the heart; for no brooding Spirit has infused into it the principle of vitality, or gifted it with the power to struggle with innate depravity.

NOTE 13
THE POLICE OF BURMAH.

"Soon after this, the native Christians in Burmah Proper, were called to endure violent persecutions."—page 116.

The government of Burmah is an absolute monarchy—life, liberty, and property, being at the unlimited and unquestioned disposal of the sovereign. There is not a life throughout the realm of so much value, that one will venture, for its sake, to resist the slightest nod of the king—no person so illustrious, but he is liable to be seized at any moment, and without the form of a trial—without even knowing of what crime he is accused, hurried away to prison or to death.

About a year since, an Armenian merchant, who had resided during twenty years at Ava, was roused from his sleep at midnight by the terrifying summons, "The King calls!" "Why has he called? how have I offended?" were useless questions; he was dragged from the midst of his trembling family, to prison, and confined in the stocks. Here he remained for about two weeks, when he was hurried to the river, thrust into a boat, and sentenced to perpetual banishment. His wife and children being native subjects of the king, were not permitted to accompany him. He subsequently learned, though incidentally, that he was accused of being in correspondence with the English; the grounds of the suspicion being his receipt of a Calcutta newspaper!

Private property is not only subject to taxation, but is liable, at any moment, to be demanded for the public good, or seized, on some trivial or false pretence, by individual officers of government. An appearance of wealth places a man at the mercy of the brood of harpies, who, in the character of rulers, are palsying the energies of the nation; so every man puts on the semblance of poverty, and steals away, like a murderer at midnight, trembling in every limb, to bury his money and jewels in the earth. Such is the Savings' Bank, which rewards the industry of the Burman; and happy is he if no wily watcher removes the carefully matched sods roofing his money-vault, and leaves him as poor as he seems. The monarch is the only landed-proprietor throughout the realm. He gives his vassals permission to build on his spacious grounds; but they have no guaranty of permanence in their possessions—the house which they build, with themselves, their families, and all things that other men are accustomed to call their own, being the undisputed property of the king, and entirely at his sovereign disposal.

The granting of offices under government is the especial prerogative of the monarch; and is the source of great gain to his favorites—as a candidate must pay his way through them, before his petition can reach the ear of royalty. A man will thus lavish all that he possesses to obtain the shelter of an official umbrella; and when the coveted prize is won, he enters upon his office, with the unscrupulous avidity of a gaunt and hungry wolf, seeking his prey. By the time he is so fully gorged that he can afford some little abatement of his cruelty and oppression, a rival stands ready to supersede him; and he must make a fresh and vigorous effort, to obtain the means of again bribing his way up to the notice of his sovereign. It is impossible to convey an idea of the abuse of power which this system engenders. Men lie down upon their pillows at night, with no feeling of security; and, by day, they walk the streets in suspicion and distrust, shrinking even from an act of kindness, as though they read equal danger in a smile as in a frown. One of the vice-governors of Rangoon, two years since, named, from his sanguinary disposition, the Bloody Ray-woon, was fertile in alluring, as well as cruel expedients. Sometimes, while a victim was suspended by the ankles, with his head downward, and writhing in agony from an accumulation of sufferings, a woman of gentle countenance and pitying voice, would step in and plead earnestly for his release. All but the poor sufferer had practiced their different parts so frequently that they knew them perfectly well; and so there would be demurring and persuasion, till at last a fine was imposed, which the woman kindly paid, taking a note of hand from the grateful and overjoyed victim. The next act in the drama was arrest for debt, a suit at law, which swelled the original amount to a sum beyond the debtor's means, and finally he was sold into slavery, the profits of the whole accruing to the vice-governor.

Every government man has a train of followers and attendants, who serve him without wages, and act as jackals to scent the prey, their own subsistence depending on their vigilance. Hence numerous stratagems to entrap the unsuspecting. An Englishman lately saw, at Rangoon, an intelligent, respectable looking Burmese woman, meanly clad, and carrying water on the wharf. Her countenance and manner appeared so little in unison with her employment, that he addressed her with some curiosity.

"This work is very hard for you, mother."

"Yes," she answered, with a sigh; "but I must do as I am bidden now; I am a slave—only a poor slave!"

"Indeed! you do not appear like a slave."

"Like what, then, do I appear?" she inquired, with some bitterness, glancing down on her coarse dress and weary limbs.

A few soothing words elicited her history—a very common one in Rangoon. She was proceeding to market one day, with vegetables from her little garden, when she was accosted by a stranger, who said he wished to purchase. He was unable, however, to please himself; and, after some little delay, he allowed her to pass on. She had proceeded only a short distance, when he suddenly called out to her that he had changed his mind, and would purchase. She returned, and lowered the basket from her head; and the man began to make his selections. Suddenly he paused, drew back, as though in consternation, then snatched something from the bottom of her basket, and thrust it into her face, crying, "Heh, you! You use *this*, do you?" It was a bit of opium—an article prohibited by government. The woman was immediately dragged away to prison and the stocks, fined heavily, and herself and children sold into slavery to pay the fine.

"It is certainly a hard case—but then you broke the laws," remarked the listener.

"I! never! I never used opium in my life!"

"How, then, came it in your basket?"

The woman looked about her cautiously, then lowered her voice. "*They* know better than I. They pretended not to believe me; but they knew all about it! Oh, there are many people here as ill-used and as miserable as I am."

Boodhism, the national religion of Burmah, is rigidly supported by the authority of the king; and every departure from the faith of Gaudama is visited upon the daring misbeliever with unrelenting rigor. From time to time, philosophers have arisen from among the people, who have ventured to teach new doctrines, or give a new interpretation to old ones; but they do not long escape the eagle-eyed executors of the king's will; and the heresy must end either in recantation or in death.

The position of foreigners is somewhat different. Though the haughty monarch is troubled with few humane or generous scruples on their behalf, he does not consider them his vassals; and their condition, compared with that of the native population, is one of enviable freedom. Romanists, Armenians, and Mahometans, are permitted to worship according to their different creeds, without molestation; and may even introduce their Burmese wives and half-cast children within the pale of their several churches. A Protestant community would, of course, be allowed similar privileges. It is only when they come in the pitying spirit of their Master, and attempt to propagate his pure and peaceful doctrines, that they meet with opposition. Proselytism, either by the distribution of books, or by public or private teaching, is strictly prohibited; and the lightest penalty which a missionary incurs, when he attempts to spread the glad news of salvation is banishment from the realm; while his little band of disciples broken, hunted down, and scattered, is left a prey to those whose tender mercies are cruel. And! since the practice of bringing *innocent* persons under the ban of the law is studied as an art, what favor can a man, guilty of embracing the prohibited religion of Jesus Christ, expect to receive? Beggary or slavery, for his family—for himself, imprisonment, torture, and death, protracted by such sufferings as he knows his countrymen are peculiarly expert in inflicting, stare him continually in the face. The secret baptism by night, in the still shadow of closely-sheltering trees—the stolen prayer-meeting, when two or three trembling hearts venture to relieve themselves in subdued, half-whispered pleadings, while they dare not raise the song of praise—the hidden treasure of books, read by stealth, and warily concealed again—each of these is fraught with such danger, as no man, save he whose strength is in the Almighty, would have the courage or hardihood to brave. Yet is there one such little band of well-known worshippers in Burmah now; while the number of the altars which may have been secretly erected to the living God, in the numerous towns and villages, lining the fair banks of the Irrawaddy, can be known alone in heaven.

NOTE 14
THE GOLDEN BALANCE.

" . . . The room where I sit all the day with my Peguan translator."—page 118.

"It is a glorious thought to the Christian, that he may still add jewels to his Master's crown, when his voice is hushed in the grave."—page 143.

SINCE THESE NOTES WERE IN course of preparation, a middle-aged man, of sober aspect and respectable appearance, came to the pastor of the church to ask for baptism. He spoke the Burmese imperfectly, and it was soon ascertained that he was a Peguan, from the vicinity of Bangkok, in Siam.

"Why do you wish to be baptized?" inquired the pastor.

"I believe in the Lord Jesus Christ; and I wish to enter his religion, and obey his commands."

"How do you know that this is one of his commands?"

"I have read about it in the 'Book of Truth.'"

"How did you first become acquainted with the religion of Jesus Christ?"

"Before I came to this region, a countryman of mine chanced to mention a wonderful little book, which a foreign teacher at Bangkok had given him; and I had the curiosity to procure and read it. I have never worshipped an idol since."

"Indeed! what book was it?"

"The Golden Balance."

The conversation for several moments ceased; for the wheel of time was thrown back too suddenly to admit of any concealment of emotion. The translation of the Golden Balance was one of the earliest of Mrs. Judson's efforts in the Peguan; and the stranger, unconsciously, sat beneath the very roof, where she had toiled for his salvation. There had the fingers, now moldering in a distant grave, given wings to the precious seed, which floated away over vale and mountain, river and woodland, to drop into the soil prepared for it by the Holy Spirit.

After due examination, and the usual preliminaries, the man was admitted to baptism; and the ordinance was administered close beside her former home. The Peguan translator, she so often mentions, now a thin, pale, stooping old man, appearing always in russet tunic and sombre-hued waist-cloth, looked on at the scene; and the duty was performed by the hands she would have chosen above all others, for administering this sacred rite to one of her spiritual children; but she, who would have been the most joyful of all the spectators, was not there. The bristling pines of the north shake their tasseled branches above the snows of her fathers' home; and the crested hoopoo-bird, seeking the golden banana and white flowering cocoa of the south, wings its way across her children's graves; while far away from either scene, upon a rock-bound island, which never felt the pressure of her tread, she is left to her lonely sleep. But by the labor of her hand and pen—by the labor of her lips, engraved on many a throbbing heart—by her prayers—and by the fragrance that clings about her memory, she is living and laboring still.

NOTE 15
THE MOTHER'S STRENGTH.

"The long letter which accompanied little George to his future guardians, . . . would, doubtless, unfold a system of maternal management, which," etc.—page 128.

Though much inquiry has been made for this letter, it has not yet been found; but the key to its author's system of management is within the reach of every reader.

"I have one request to make," said Mrs. Boardman to her dying husband, "it is that you would pray much for George, during your few remaining days." Years passed away, and trials were again clustering around the pathway of the sorrowing wife; and again she preferred her request. "I wish, my love, you would pray for one object in particular—that I may be assisted in communicating divine truth to the minds of these little immortals." Still time hurried on, and the wife and mother was herself shorn of her strength; and, with only half her family of little ones about her, away upon the restless ocean, she lay in her cabin dying. She had done what she could—she had instructed and disciplined—she had given sympathy, and love, and prayers, and tears; and she was about turning from all her anxieties and toils to rest in the Saviour's bosom. Surely, her work is ended now, and she may contemplate the glories before her without one backward glance. But no; not yet. Eternity will be long enough for rest; and her failing breath and fleeting moments are too precious to be wasted. "During her last days," says the solitary watcher by her bedside, "she spent much of her time in praying for the early conversion of her children;" and he adds, "may her living and her dying prayers draw down the blessing of God on their bereaved heads."

The children for whom so much praying breath was expended are scattered far—separated by "stormy seas, and the wide world's expanse;" but could the sainted mother look upon them in their respective homes, she would find occasion for renewed gratitude to him, who is peculiarly the orphan's friend. The son, who was for many years her "only one," long previous to her death, had rejoiced her heart by giving evidence of early piety; and it is hoped that his health will be sufficiently good to enable him to complete the collegiate course upon which he has entered. Her daughter is a pupil in Bradford Academy, so well known as the intellectual nursery of Ann Hasseltine and Harriet Atwood; and has found an enviable home, with the pious and highly-accomplished sisters of the former. The two sons, who accompanied her in her last voyage, have succeeded

George Boardman in the affectionate interest and watchful solicitude of Doct. and Mrs. Calvin Newton, of Worcester, Mass.; and of the three whom she left to the tender and sympathizing care of her missionary sisters in Burman, one preceded her to heaven, while the others move in the places hallowed by her former prayers, beneath their father's eye. It was in connection with these two little boys, that the propriety of noting the birthdays of children, by some little ceremony, to remind them of the flight of time, became, not long since, the subject of conversation.

"How did their own mother observe the return of these days?" was at length inquired.

"She made them seasons of fasting," was the reply; "and spent most of the day in her closet, either alone or in company with the child, giving such instructions as she thought best adapted to its age and character."

NOTE 16
BURMESE POETRY.

"Her hymns in Burmese, about twenty in number, are probably the best in our Chapel Hymn Book."—page 142.

The structure of the Burmese language is peculiarly favorable to poetical composition. Being monosyllabic, it is capable of every variety of metrical disposition; and the rhyme is still farther assisted by a multiplicity of euphonic expletives, and chiming increments. The art of poetry is cultivated to a high degree, especially in the vicinity of the court; and in addition to dramatic compositions, and voluminous epics, there are odes, elegies, and dirges, boat songs, and cart songs, and love songs, chiming proverbs, and epigrams without number. The nursery is also well supplied with its own peculiar literature; and the women lounge idly in the shade, chanting, all day long, some simple rhyme; as,

Nan lee ma kōng,
Ka-do pōng!
Nan lee ma wah,
Moung loo hlah

I weary not of smelling (or kissing[1]) thee,
Bundle of musk!
I am not satisfied with kissing thee,
Beautiful boy!

The language, from a sort of inherent piquancy, is well adapted to short, pithy sayings, and epigrams, which, however, mostly lose their point in translation. A common proverb runs thus:

Youk-yah bōng,
Let yōng;
Ming-mah bōng.
San-dōng.

The glory of a man,
His arm!
The glory of a woman,
Her top-knot.

The hymns composed by the missionaries, being adapted to our sacred music, are mostly constructed on the principles of English poetry, from which that of the Burmans differs very widely. There are two or three exceptions, however, in the Chapel Hymn Book, of which the following, from a funeral hymn, is a specimen, and may serve to give some idea of Burmese versification. This hymn appears in the English dress of lines and stanzas—a division which the Burmans never make, their poetry being written like prose. The

1 These two words are synonymous—kissing with the lips being unknown to the Burmans.

italics will show the syllable on which the rhyme falls.

Mike sway kyoon *wen*,
Then gyaing *twen* wai;
Kyeet *ken* tah *shay* loon lo *nay;*
Myay pau hnyeen *pan*,
Hloon ket *tan* swah;
Bay *kyan* myah *lay*, kyōng yah *kyay*.

This is one among numerous modes of poetical composition, all of which, however, are but slight deviations from the two great principles, which seem to lie at the foundation of all Burmese poetry—the tetrasyllabic measure, and triple rhyme.

The following translation of one of Mrs. Judson's hymns, may be admitted as a tolerable specimen of her labors in this department; though it has been found difficult to preserve the simplicity of the original; and the sentiments lose much of their force by being transferred to another language, and a different scene. The first two stanzas, especially, convey a distinct and positive meaning to Burmese converts, which can never be appreciated by those who worship God beneath genial skies, with "none to molest or make them afraid."

DIVINE ASSISTANCE IMPLORED.

When, like torrents, swiftly rushing,
Foes arise in every place,
Mocking, persecuting, crushing,
Oh, defend us, God of Grace!

When the friends, that used to cherish,
Drive us from our homes so dear,
Parents send us forth to perish,
Then, Oh God of Love, be near!

When, with subtle words beguiling,
Satan comes his arts to wield,
Like a serpent, twining, wiling,
God of Mercy, be our shield!

When with pale disease we languish,
Or, on beds of suffering laid,
Toss in restless, burning anguish,
God of Pity, lend thine aid!

When, our earthly vision failing,
Death's dark realm before us lies,
Far from scenes of woe and wailing,
Bear us, God of Paradise!

The first stanza of the above hymn, is here inserted in the original Burman character:

။အသနားတော်ခံသီခြင်း။

ကျေးဇူးရှင်ကိုယုံကြည်ချစ်လေ၊
နှိပ်စက်ညှဉ်းဆဲကဲ့ရဲ့ခြင်း။
ဖြစ်ရေစီးလို၊ရန်သူထလေ့။
စောင့်မတော်မူပါသခင်။

NOTE 17
BOODH.

"Then gird thine armor on, Love,
Nor faint thou by the way,
Till Boodh shall fall, and Burmah's sons
Shall own Messiah's sway."—page 150.

A Boodh is a being, who, by virtue of the voluntary performance of certain austerities, becomes the object of supreme adoration throughout the universe, and, from that state, passes into annihilation.[1] He has been, like all other beings, transmigrating through various stages of existence from eternity; but upon receiving, through a predecessor, some intimation of the high destiny that awaits him, he enters upon a course of sacrifices and sufferings, the duration of which it is impossible to compute. As the length of the life of man after the deluge was gradually diminished, some suppose that it will be increased as gradually, till, during the approaching millennium, it will be once more measured by centuries instead of scores. Something like this, though on a far more magnificent scale, is the theory of the Boodhists. They believe that the common age of man has been thus fluctuating from eternity, like the ebb and flow of the sea. There is a time when the "years of his life" are only ten; but they continue swelling, gradually, till they amount to one hundred quadrillions of quadrigintillions, a number designated by a unit and one hundred and forty cyphers. When man arrives at this age of longevity, which the Burmans term an *a-then-kyay*, his age decreases, with the same imperceptible slowness, until it is again reduced to the term of ten years. This inconceivable stretch of time, for which the English language has no name, and before which, figures become useless, constitutes what the Burmans call an Intermediate Period. Sixty-four of these Intermediate Periods complete one Cardinal Period, and four Cardinal Periods one Grand Period or Cycle, termed a *Kam-bah*, (Sanscrit, *Kalpa*.) Gaudama, the last Boodh, toiled, to obtain his divinity, through four *a-then-kyays* of these Grand Cycles, with the comparatively trifling addition of one hundred thousand Kam-bahs at the end. He was finally

1 This being must not be confounded with the Boodh of Hindoo Mythology, one of the ten incarnations of Vishnu. That very disreputable incarnation, made to synchronize with the last Boodh, was, doubtless, fabricated by the Brahmins, for the purpose of degrading the divinity of their powerful rivals to a level with their own gods, the Nats of Burmah.

born of human parents, 624 years before Christ; and spent the early part of his life amid the voluptuous splendors of an eastern court, being the only son of a powerful Indian monarch. At the age of twenty-nine he renounced royalty, with all its attractions, among which a harem of eighty thousand oriental beauties was not the least. Abandoning his only son, and the wife who had accompanied him through countless ages—being a tigress when he was a tiger, a doe when he was a deer, and the queen of heaven or hell, as he wielded the scepter of either realm—he fled into the wilderness. There he spent six years in practicing austerities of unprecedented severity, after which he found himself invested with a divine nature, and thus became the supreme object of worship. He flourished as a Boodh, until eighty years of age; when he died, and attained *Nigban*, or annihilation.[1] His claims to supreme adoration, however, extend to five thousand years after his extinction. Thus the temples and sacred groves are crowded with his images; and pagodas are everywhere erected over some portion of his reputed relics, which are as miraculously plentiful, as the fragments of the "true cross" among the devotees of Rome.

To give a more definite idea of the nature of a Boodh, it will be necessary to enter upon a brief outline of the system of worlds. The Grand Cycle, termed a Kam-bah, comprehends one entire revolution of nature, or the age of a world. The Period begins with the destruction of the old world, by the three elements, fire, air and water. During the first of the four Cardinal Periods, which constitute a Kam-bah, the earth is enveloped in a conflagration. During the second Period, the flames are struggling with roaring winds and dashing waters; and the third, is occupied in processes of re-organization. At the beginning of the fourth Period, a little spot of earth

1 The word *Nigban*, is undoubtedly derived from the same root as the Sanscrit *Nirvan*, which implies absorption in Deity; but the Boodhists, so far from adopting this theory of Brahmivism, would regard it with horror. The idea of any being superior to a Boodh, who should receive his divine essence, would be in the opinion, blasphemous; and the only meaning they attach to the word *Nigban*, is simple annihilation.

appears in the midst of the limitless waste of waters; and the spirits congregated in the invisible regions, that have escaped the conflagration, bend their heads to gaze down upon it with intense interest. A magnificent lily springs up from the centre of the mound; and if it blossoms, they are filled with joy; for the period is to be blest by the advent of as many Boodhs as the lily stem bears flowers. Most frequently it is barren; in which case, the period is full of gloom, and all creatures are degraded and miserable. The present Kambah is of an extraordinarily high order, the emblematic lily having borne five blossoms. Four Boodhs—Kek-Ku-than, Gau-na-gong, Kat-tha-ba, and Gau-da-ma[1]—have already flourished, and passed into annihilation; and another is yet to be developed. The age of man is now on the ebb, and will continue to decrease, till reduced to the term of ten years; then it will gradually rise again, until it attains the enormous height of an a-then-kyay of years. During the next ebb, when the age of man is diminished to a hundred thousand years, A-re-ma-day,[2] the fifth Boodh, will appear, and flourish eighty thousand years.

As the waters continue to recede, the beautiful results of processes carried on during the previous period, become visible. The Myeen-mo Mount stands in the centre of the rising system, encircled by seven graduated ranges of mountains, which are separated from each other by seven broad belts of water. Beyond these, in the direction of the cardinal points of the compass, appear four large islands, around each of which cluster five hundred smaller ones; and the whole is encompassed by a wall of incalculable height and magnitude. The base of the central mountain is inhabited by five races of monsters; and above these, midway from the base, and extending thence to the summit, is the first celestial region. The summit, a beautiful plain one hundred and twenty thousand miles in extent, and surrounded by high walls, constitutes the second celestial region; and over this, ranged one above another, at unequal distances, are

1 All accented on the first and third syllables, thus:—*Kek*-ku-*than*, etc.

2 Accented on the second and fourth syllables:—A-*re*-ma-*day*.

four similar inferior heavens, and twenty superior ones, the four highest of which are immaterial and invisible. The distance, from the foot of the mountain to the highest heaven, is eight hundred and sixty-four millions of miles. The Myeen-mo Mount is reared on three immense rocks, so arranged as to leave a concave space in the centre; and this place is occupied by a race of beings resembling the Titans of old, who have been banished from the celestial regions. Below this, are ranged eight hells, one immediately beneath the other, and extending through a layer of earth one hundred and twenty thousand miles in depth. The earth rests on a rocky stratum of the same depth, beneath which is a continually restless flood of water; and still below this, a similar body of air, by the mighty force of whose continued action and re-action, the whole structure is supported.

At the commencement of the new organization just described, several glorious beings, while gliding through the upper regions of air, inhale a delicious perfume, which they trace down to the southernmost of the four large islands. This they find, as it emerged from the waters, fresh and beautiful; and they delay their return to dally with its attractions, till, in process of time, they become so gross, that the glory which illuminated their bodies is extinguished, and they are left in utter darkness. At this crisis, the sun and moon very opportunely appear, and commence their revolutions around the central mount, on a level with the summit of the middle range of encircling mountains. The celestial visitants, having lost the power of traversing air, as formerly, are compelled to make their homes below. Here they continue to deteriorate, until they undergo important physical changes, and the propagation of the race of man commences.

Each of the four large islands is one hundred and twenty thousand miles in extent, but they vary in form, being fashioned like the faces of the beings who inhabit them. The Southern Island, shaped like the human face, is the earth on which we dwell, and the only spot where a Boodh can be developed, or from which any being can pass into annihilation. The chance of becoming an inhabitant of earth is, as though a needle, tossed from the summit of Myeen-mo Mount, should strike with its point the point of some particular needle planted on the Southern Island; or as though a mass of fragments, which are cast into an ocean, drifted thousands of miles, and stranded on a hundred coasts, should, by the careless winds and tossing billows, again be brought together. There are, therefore, few greater boons in the gift of fate, than that of being born a man, on this favored isle.

Ten thousand systems of worlds, like the one above described, each with its central mount, its heavens and its hells, its mountains and moats, its islands and outer wall, are destroyed and reproduced at same time. The influence of a Boodh can extend over a trillion; while his omniscience, when he so wills it, embraces the vast infinitude of systems, which are stretched out on a limitless plain, in as close contact with each other as their circular walls will admit.

The jurisdiction exercised by a Boodh is neither that of a lawgiver, nor a judge. He is a mere religious teacher, explaining the immutable laws of duty and destiny, and persuading men to perform meritorious deeds; but he has no power to forgive sin, or avert the suffering, which is its inevitable consequence. Most of his time is passed in a species of ecstatic reverie, peculiar to himself; but he will "preach," when invited, or when suitable occasions present themselves; and he frequently travels from place to place, in search of meritorious persons, who need his aid on their way to annihilation. He is insusceptible of human passions, emotions or sympathies, though liable to physical suffering, disease, and death. Omniscience, and that of an imperfect character, is the only attribute of the true God, which is claimed for him; and with the exception of ability to perform a minor class of miracles, he has no more power than any other man. Like all beings, he is a creature of destiny; and even after he has entered upon his Boodhship, is not exempt from the penalty of sins committed in a former state of existence.

To such a system of religion, which owns no living God, and

counts immortality a curse—a system, brilliant with many a glowing fragment of sin-shattered mind, and hoary with the honored rime of antiquity—millions, and hundreds of millions of our race are at this very moment clinging, as their only hope. And, in order to effect the overthrow of this system, together with Brahminism and Mahometanism, the Church of Christ must awake to the employment of her highest energies, and must put forth her mightiest efforts. It is no trifling foe, with which she has to contend—no light skirmishing with the unarmed few upon the outskirts of the army, which is to engage her strength; but she is to attack the very heart of the fortress, and grapple with the Prince of Darkness on his throne. Every Christian will thank God for the wonders he is performing among the Greenlanders the South Sea Islanders, the West Indian Negroes, and the Karens of Burmah; but no discriminating Christian will be unduly elated when he considers that such results have been limited to comparatively small tribes, destitute of a systematic religion, a national literature, and even a written language; and, therefore, presenting few obstacles to Christianization. The great battle of the Lord is to be fought upon a different field. The haughty priesthood, the imposing ceremonies, the spacious temples, and magnificent pagodas, that are the pride and glory of those nations on which the heavy curse of idolatry is resting, are not so easily demolished. But demolished they must be, eventually; and even now is the work begun. The clang of Gospel armor, from the plains of India, mingles with the noise of the battery, that has commenced its daring play upon the walls of China; and the stroke of the armorer's hammer, which never ceases in the borders of Burmah and Siam, is echoed from choice citadels, that are springing up beneath the curve of the Moslem crescent. From other lands, also—lands crimsoned with the blood of martyrs, or blackened by infidelity—from the abodes of the wandering sons of Israel, from dark-browed Africa, and from the wilds of America, the axe of the sturdy pioneer is ringing, and the trumpet of the Lord is pealing forth a battle-call. We are standing on the vestibule of a resplendently glorious era. The angel "having the everlasting Gospel to preach," is already "in the midst of heaven," and we hear the rushing of his mighty wings;—the Church is shaking off the drowsy dust of ages, polishing her weapons, and spreading her banner to the breeze;—the word of command has sounded from the walls of heaven; and there are sure indications, that the immutable promises of Jehovah are hastening to their accomplishment. Already the Morning Star has risen on thousands and tens of thousands "sitting in darkness, and in the region and shadow of death;" and although the twilight is yet gray about us, there is a deepening glow upon the sky, sure usher of advancing day. Courage, lone laborer!—Of the myriads who have lived and passed from earth before thee, who so blest as thou? Courage!—Each well-directed blow of thine is destined to reverberate through eternity; and every ray shed from thy Gospel lamp, speeds away as the mountain-rill to the ocean, swelling the flood of radiance, which is ere long to sweep over the entire earth. Then, at the rising of the Sun of Righteousness, shall the nations clap their hands in gladness, and the redeemed and renovated race of man burst forth in one universal shout: "HALLELUJAH! HALLELUJAH! THE LORD GOD OMNIPOTENT REIGNETH!"

Made in United States
Orlando, FL
01 June 2022

18394300R00118